1984 BRITISH OPEN

1979 BRITISH OPEN

1988 BRITISH OPEN

1983 MASTERS

1980 MASTERS

Natural GOLF

by

SEVE BALLESTEROS

with JOHN ANDRISANI

Editorial Consultant KEN BOWDEN

Illustrated by DOM LUPO

Swing sequence photographs by LEONARD KAMSLER

Atheneum New York 1988

Atheneum
Macmillan Publishing Company
866 Third Avenue, New York, N.Y. 10022
Collier Macmillan Canada, Inc.

Library of Congress Cataloging-in-Publication Data

Ballesteros, Severiano.
Natural golf / by Seve Ballesteros with John Andrisani;
illustrated by Dom Lupo.
p. cm.
ISBN 0-689-11846-5
1. Golf. I. Andrisani, John. II. Title.
GV965.B19 1988
796.352'3--dc19 88-18744
CIP

Designed by Robert Michaels

10 9 8 7 6 5 4 3 2 1

Printed in the United States of America

For my father,
Baldomero Ballesteros Presmanes

Contents

Natural GOLF

Foreword

The first time I saw Seve Ballesteros play golf was during the 1976 British Open Championship, contested over the famed Royal Birkdale links, near Southport, in England. Back then, Ballesteros was only nineteen years old, a mere child by professional standards; yet he displayed such unmistakable signs of golfing maturity on the course that, after his second-place finish, it was obvious that this flamboyant young Spaniard was anything but a flash in the pan.

Even then, Seve appeared to me to employ the simplest, most natural-looking, rhythmic, repeatable swing of perhaps any pro I'd ever seen—Sam Snead included! The fearlessness and fieriness in his eyes seemed another harbinger of superstardom, for in my time only golfers such as Ben Hogan, Arnold Palmer, Jack Nicklaus, and Tom Watson have possessed that special "look." And then, of course, there was the youngster's almost uncanny flair for trouble shots, which instantly made him the favorite of the fans.

Ballesteros's go-for-broke style of play was very reminiscent of Palmer, who, in his heyday, also drove par-fours and invariably fired the ball dead at the flagstick from both on and far off the fairway. Nevertheless, whereas Arnie sized things up and set up quickly then seemed to slash at the ball instinctively, Seve meticulously studied each course situation with the intensity of an artist eyeing a new sheet of white canvas, always using his strong imaginative powers to paint a vivid picture of the desired shot in his mind's eye. Then, swinging in his own special way, he masterly executed feat after feat of astonishing shotmaking magic.

One stroke in particular, a deft, delicately played pitch-and-run that Seve miraculously bounced and rolled between two treacherous greenside traps stiff to the pin at the seventy-second hole, provoked even the most blasé among the huge press corps to immediately hail the young Spaniard a shotmaking genius.

Three years later, I saw Ballesteros win his first major championship—the 1979 British Open at Royal Lytham & St. Anne's. And, while working in England from 1980 to 1982 as assistant editor of *Golf Illustrated*, I traveled to many tournaments where I was able to track Seve's competitive progress on both the European and American circuits. However, it wasn't until I joined America's *Golf* magazine as senior editor, and started working with Seve on instructional articles for that publication in 1983, that I began to truly get inside this man and his method.

Initially, I was very suspect of Seve's self-learned, principally right-sided technique, for, without exception, every previous golfer of true stature was either a totally left-sided or a two-sided swinger. Moreover, professionals who *thought* they swung one way when in fact they swung another were legion.

However, after watching many Ballesteros victories, and listening to him for hours at a time as he verbally dissected and then pieced together his technique, such doubts totally evaporated. Seve did, and still does, employ an essentially right-sided swing that requires no muscular contortion and a minimum amount of mental discipline to keep on track. Once Seve convinced me that his method of swinging a golf club was, indeed, the most natural for right-handers, and thus very easy to learn and repeat, I agreed to collaborate with him on the creation of this book.

Despite his hectic worldwide tournament schedule, Ballesteros has given 100 percent commitment to the work, meticulously ensuring that every detail of his technique was correctly interpreted and communicated in easy-to-follow fashion.

Everything Seve Ballesteros knows about playing golf—from the fundamentals of setting up, to the finest points of swinging, through the whole lexicon of shotmaking and scoring—is here to help you either to learn the game from scratch, or to play it better and more enjoyably.

I think you will find that one of the most appealing aspects of this book is its honesty.

Seve concedes that attempting to replicate the Ballesteros technique exactly is unlikely to produce precisely the same results in another golfer. On the other hand, he believes very strongly that his natural way of swinging will get the great majority of golfers to return the clubface squarely to the ball *most* of the time—provided they are willing to work seriously at understanding and mentally ingraining a set of bedrock principles, then permanently implanting each one into their muscle memory through diligent practice. And that, of course, when all the fat is boiled off, is the *realistic* goal that all golfers should constantly be striving for.

Whether you're a novice looking to play simply at a nonembarrassing level, or an ambitious golfer who feels that finding his "true swing" is even more difficult than discovering his "true self," this book will be of enormous help. However, in your eagerness to get off to a flying start, heed Seve's advice and do a little soul-searching on your own. In other words, it's a good idea to work within the basic framework set down in this book, but it's an even better idea to be open to making slight adjustments, particularly in such areas as ball position, width of stance, and length of swing, every time you play. Why?

Because none of us are machines, we can never expect to swing exactly the same way we did the last time we played, especially if that last time was last week, last month, or last year! Consequently, only by "listening to our bodies" and making the minor changes they suggest in our setup and swing on the practice tee, before play, can we accommodate our inevitable changes in bodily feel, flexibility, strength, and so forth.

Personally, I think the publication of *Natural Golf* is perfectly timed, in that an ever-growing number of young and young-at-heart people are taking up this great game. To me, there could be no better way to begin than with the techniques of the golfer most experts consider to be the greatest in the world at the present time.

John Andrisani

Introduction

I've had books written about me before, most notably a biography by Dudley Doust, entitled *Seve: The Young Champion* (1982) and *Seve* (1986), a pictorial essay by the photographer Phil Sheldon. Both provide good glimpses into my golfing development, and also chronicle through words and pictures my finer and not-so-fine moments as a tournament professional. However, this book is the first I have produced myself, and the first time I have attempted to set down in totality the techniques upon which my play is based.

I had seriously considered setting my theories down on paper before now, but kept procrastinating because of my heavy commitments in other areas around the world, most notably tournament golf. Also, I wanted to be absolutely sure that my essentially right-sided techniques were truly as simple and effective as they seemed to me, which could best be established by a good competitive record.

The idea of golf being a left-handed game for right-handers remains a preposterous premise to me. Because the right hand is the part of the anatomy closest to the clubhead, I've always believed that it should be the principal conduit of golfing feel and control. However, to be absolutely sure this was also true of others, a little while back I put the technique to the test at the Real Club de Golf de Pedreña, near my home in Spain, using a group of juniors and adults, including some senior men and women, as "guinea pigs."

I started novices off with my method of swinging, and had the more experienced players with varying handicaps gradually switch to it. When we finished up, almost unanimously the two dozen students felt that, if I were to write an instuctional book on the techniques I'd taught them, it would bring a great deal of increased pleasure from the game to golfers all over the world. That shot of enthusiam, plus my own desire to give something back to a game that has been so great to me, was the incentive I needed to create what you are now holding in your hands.

Actually, the process of writing the book was very analogous to the development of my professional career, in that both took a lot of patience and perseverance, plus much support from others, to be fully realized.

Much of what you will read here relates to the golfing theories and methods I developed over many years by personal trial and error. I have also given credit to those childhood chums who inspired me in their own way during our youthful competitions.

Perhaps not enough has been said about the influence on my game of my three older brothers, Baldomero, Manuel, and Vicente. All three have been constant sources of analysis, suggestion, and encouragement. We basically all play golf today with the same approach to the fundamentals, thus at one time or another each has been instrumental in helping me achieve breakthroughs in my game, or in regaining form after a difficult spell.

In particular, Vicente, who nowadays travels with me to most golf tournaments, has a deep knowledge of my techniques. So that he can get a close-up view of my form from day to day under competitive conditions, he often will caddie for me. During the year he also works countless hours with me on the practice tee, to the point where he has become a most valuable coach. A talented professional golfer in his own right, and a gifted teacher, Vicente is today the person I consult whenever I have questions about my game, and thus in an indirect way has contributed significantly to this book.

Finally, I owe special thanks to John Andrisani, an excellent golfer and a fine writer who has become a good friend. John worked long and laboriously to try to set down my techniques simply and clearly, but completely and graphically enough to allow golfers of all levels to grasp and master them as easily as possible.

I hope you enjoy the book, and that it helps you get more fun from the wonderful game of golf.

Seve Ballesteros

PART 1

ON LEARNING GOLF

Chapter 1

THE BENEFITS OF TEACHING YOURSELF

I'm constantly called a "natural," as if I were born with a golf club in my hand and a scratch-handicap swing. That's not true. I wasn't innately blessed with the skill to smash a tee shot three hundred yards, the talent to hit an iron shot stiff to the flagstick, or the knack to knock a monster putt in the hole. No one is.

Yet there is no mystery in how every fine golfer became good at the game. It's a matter of fact. The only way a person can possibly reach his or her golfing goals is to build a simple, *repeatable* swing based on sound fundamentals. After that, golf is mostly about practice, practice, practice.

The harsh reality, that systematic practice is essential, may sink into the heads of most amateurs but rarely into their hearts, where it counts the most. Deep down, the weekend golfer knows that practice is a long-term investment, involving much time and effort. And that's the problem. Excuses for "passing" on practice are as many and varied as bad shots on Saturday mornings. And yet the sad irony is that every golfer desperately wants to play better.

Some golfers I've been paired with in Pro-Am tournaments have been very honest about this. They argue that devoting hours to practice is no guarantee that they will hold onto a sound swing from week to week, or from day to day, or even from shot to shot. I chuckle every time I hear that comment—or, rather, rationalization—for two reasons. First, I once felt the same way. Second, there's some truth in what they say.

Sometimes, getting up in the morning, I feel fit as a fiddle for golf, and on the practice tee I hit the ball just super. Then, on the course, my swing sours and my mental pictures and images become muddled. On days like that, my Spanish blood runs hot, so I have to work extra hard to simmer down and stop the score from skyrocketing.

On another occasion, I'll fly across the Atlantic, arrive at a strange hotel feeling tired, and, after a restless night, wolf down too much breakfast. Warming up, I hit the ball poorly and miss putts. Then, out on the course—bingo!—a record score.

My point: Golf is a very mysterious and puzzling game, causing much frustration for *all* who play it at *every* level.

The golf swing is far too complex to nail down to a science. Starting from a static position and swinging the club back, up and then down so that its face strikes the ball squarely and solidly while traveling at great speed requires an extremely precise coordination of the mind and body. Because of the interplay of so many variables, it's no wonder the game is so difficult for the average player. Pressure, patience, routine, rhythm, metabolism, self-confidence, consciousness of score, strength, timing, tempo, and technique all play a role. So, for all of us, good swings come, and just as quickly they go.

All the same, each of us shares the same quest: to keep bad days to a minimum. Our goal is to find swing keys that will enable us to score well easily when we "have it," and to "play badly well" when we don't. In other words, we all want to develop above all else a *simple* swing, one that works effortlessly most of the time, but, when it is not quite on the track, still enables us to hit even our bad shots not too disastrously. Then, it's up to us to buckle down and keep our emotions under control and our thinking straight so that we can identify the high-percentage strategies, and hit to the safest spots, and thereby still make at least a decent score.

I'd like to see all golfers lower their handicaps, but I don't possess all the answers to the mysteries of the golf swing. I am no magician, capable of waving a wand so that, hey presto, suddenly having read this book you are a scratch golfer. I am a stickler for solid fundamentals, and especially for the preswing basics such as the correct grip, stance, posture, and body and clubface alignment common to all good players. However, my actual overall golf swing remains somewhat unorthodox and personal. Copying my technique to the letter is no guarantee that you will play exactly like I do.

Nevertheless, I made a commitment to myself before starting this book to try as hard as I could to *help you help yourself* to play better golf. I'd like to think that by incorporating some of my physical keys into your technique—and picking up some mental pointers, too—you will genuinely and lastingly improve at the game. However, although I can perhaps draw you to the water, I can't make you drink. Whether you choose to go my way and teach yourself, or be taught by someone else, how good a golfer you will eventually become depends finally on how much and how well you practice.

WHY PRACTICE IS SO VITAL

Unfortunately, practice never makes you perfect at golf, but practice is indispensable because it is the only way to be fully prepared for the many challenges and opportunities with which the course will present you each time you play. Try the following analogy on for size.

You never really know what to expect of life. You know you have to report to an office, or a school, or do work around the house, just as I have to arrive at a tournament site. Beyond that, lots of times each day there are surprises in store, some for the better, others for the worse. Nevertheless, the better your preparation, the better you are able to cope—whether preparation means reviewing notes for a business meeting, studying for an exam, or making out a shopping list.

Golf is as unpredictable as any other facet of life, so the same philosophy holds true: To give yourself the best possible chance of playing to your potential, you must prepare for every eventuality. That means *practice*. Now, I know only too well that very often you truly "just don't have the time." In spite of that, if you want to *really* improve, you will have to make the decision, and then the commitment, to sacrifice some of your present playing time for practice time.

Like most, I had trouble accepting this as a youngster. I was a normal boy: very impatient and insistent on doing things my own way. I was naive, too, believing that, if I simply banged out golf balls all day long, a good swing would eventually just "happen." Well, did I learn the hard way! I discovered there are no shortcuts to learning a fine golf swing. *You must lay the proper foundation*. There simply is no other way.

So, eventually, much as it hurt, I was forced to recognize that I had to learn the fundamentals, or "building blocks," of the swing, in that this was the only way I could ever hope to master the proper movements of the body and the golf club. However, rather than being tutored by a skilled instructor, as so many ambitious young Americans are today, I had no option but to teach myself by trial and error.

This process was a long and hard one, and it was slowed even more because of limited playing privileges and lack of early encouragement from my father and mother. Equipment was a problem, too. I did not have a complete set of new clubs until I was sixteen, when I turned professional. Until then, I had to make do with hand-me-downs.

I acquired my first golf club at the age of seven, a rustic model made from an old 3-iron head, with a stick I cut myself for a shaft. I used pebbles for golf balls. A year later, Manuel, the second oldest of my three brothers—all of whom are now golf professionals—gave me an authentic 3-iron and some real golf balls. But there remained some serious stumbling blocks.

Caddies at Spain's Pedreña Golf Club were allowed few liberties, so I had to practice on the beach, or in the fields behind my family's farmhouse, or in the caddie yard. And although I often watched my uncle, Ramon Sota, our country's first famous

tournament professional, and to some degree learned by imitating him, I never had a teacher to give me formal lessons.

Don't get me wrong. Learning the preswing fundamentals and the basic motions of golf from a qualified teaching professional may seem in many ways to be the ideal. However, when you teach yourself as I did, you become in time your own highly trained swing mechanic, and that skill is a truly mighty competitive asset. When you know *exactly* what makes your technique work, you can trace and fix faults on your own, even to the point of sometimes turning your game around in the middle of a tournament round.

The self-help approach also will encourage you to improvise—to try different setups and swings so that, slowly but surely, you will learn the techniques for playing a wide variety of golf shots. This is an art I picked up first by being forced to play every shot with a 3-iron. The versatility that once seeming hardship has given me in both the imagining and the physical manufacturing of strokes is today perhaps my strongest suit as a tournament golfer.

When you're your own master, you have to answer your own questions. I found that to be very good for me, because eventually it taught me all about common sense, concentration, determination, patience, and the systems and disciplines necessary to problem solving. However, being a boss carries with it heavy responsibility—in this case, to yourself. If you choose my way you will experience many highs and lows, many frustrations as well as many satisfactions. Yet if you can find the strength to get up and start over when the going gets rough, ultimately you will become a very complete and confident golfer.

I am just that today, and to say so is not braggadocio or arrogance, but simply pride in what is clearly a proven fact. Yes, I'm very proud of the finished product, the Seve Ballesteros golf game—although I'm the first to admit that there is room for improvement, and always will be.

No amount of practice will ever groom anyone to play golf to absolute perfection. But, because proper practice trains you to hit all sorts of shots, and builds confidence, it prepares you for the endless challenges involved in playing to your best potential.

THE COMMON GOAL

After all these years, I still work constantly on my swing, but these days I do it with great caution in regard to changes, to avoid getting tangled in the trendy swing theories that are always popping up, or the "Band-Aid" cures that become so tempting whenever a golfer is not playing his best.

Probably the most important lesson I learned as a kid watching topnotch golfers was that, although all share the same handful of fundamentals, no two swings are identical, *except at the most crucial point of the action—impact.*

At impact, every good player has his left hand, arm, and clubshaft lined up with the clubface, which is square to the target, solidly on the back-center of the ball, and traveling at high speed. That is *the* number one fundamental of good golf, and the principal goal we all constantly strive for in both building a swing and maintaining it.

The point is that it doesn't matter if you look like a beast before or after the hit, as long as you look like a beauty at the moment of impact.

One of the advantages of teaching yourself golf is that it gives you maximum freedom to experiment. Once you ingrain the proper preliminaries, and get a basic mental picture and sensory feel for motion, either from a teacher or from watching fine players, then you can tinker with various patterns and combinations of preparation and action until you find "your" swing, which means the one that is both fundamentally sound *and* suited to your own build, strength, and temperament.

My only criticism of modern-day teaching is that too often instructors seem to believe in just one method for everyone. The student often then suffers by not being allowed to make the most of his individual strengths, even though he may end up achieving all the precise angles and positions the teacher holds as gospel. Remember: You do not have to *look pretty* to play good, or even great, golf. All you have to do is *apply the clubface squarely to the ball at speed repetitively.*

The experimental or trial-and-error process of self-teaching that I was forced to adopt enabled me to discover a number of very reliable swing keys, such as the right-handed move I use to "trigger" the backswing. This action may not be a "classic" move, but it is a simple and, I believe, natural one, and as such it remains at the root of my technique. And I'm particularly excited about sharing it here, because I think it will help a great many others play better golf much more easily.

Throughout this book, proceeding systematically and logically, I will walk you through all the motions of my swing. We will break each one down step by step so that you can understand, completely, both the physical and mental components of my technique. At the end, if you will be selective relative to your own strengths and weaknesses—*and will practice!*—I am certain you will be a much better golfer.

DOING WHAT COMES NATURALLY

Before I touch on my number one swing key, I'd like to explain my reasons for adopting it.

The majority of teachers I've met in my travels teach "left-sided" golf. They tell students to start and then continue directing the backswing with the left side. One might instruct a student to begin by pushing off with the left foot, a second will say rotate the left hip, others recommend turning the left shoulder, while still others advise pulling or pushing the club back with the left hand, or left arm, or left hand *and* left arm.

Now, to be fair, there have always been, and there will always be, great golfers who focus to a greater or lesser degree on the left side. In fact, many of today's champions, including Tom Watson, Greg Norman, and Sandy Lyle tend to be more left-side than right-side conscious (although Jack Nicklaus has always sworn that golf is very much a *two*-sided game). However, because most of the human race is right-handed, these left-side moves very rarely come easily or naturally for most people. I don't care about the old expression, "Golf is a game of opposites." Any time you ask an individual to do something that doesn't click with his nature, it is bound to be both physically difficult and mentally confusing for him or her. That's certainly what happened to me early on, when I tried so hard and for so long to start the swing by working mostly with my left side. In fact, at one point I became so depressed that I even contemplated giving up the game entirely.

However, instead of quitting, I sat down one day and did what I call "armchair practice," a form of meditation that I still do routinely, at home or in the privacy of my hotel room. Resting quietly and breathing deeply enables me to relax and clear the mental cobwebs, so that I can more quickly get to the root of a problem and find a solution.

Noting that I performed almost all of my everyday tasks with my right hand, I decided to apply this thinking to my golf swing, and it worked. It did not work *overnight*, mind you, for the switch required a complete physical and mental overhaul. But, eventually, the change paid off royally, and I've been essentially a right-sided player ever since.

If you are right-handed, I am convinced you, too, would play golf more easily, and come much closer to your ultimate potential, with the emphasis more on your right than your left side. And it will encourage you to know that presently I see an increasing number of young players around the world putting more and more emphasis on the use of the right side in both the development and the fine-tuning of their games.

Do not go overboard, however. Having read the above, don't immediately run to the practice tee and attempt to instantly revamp your swing to a right-sided technique. Especially do not do that if you play pretty decent golf already. Remember what I told you earlier: Miracles just don't happen in this game. Everything takes time—and work.

The start of the swing is one of its most critical points. Make a faulty move as you initiate the action and the chances of correcting it later are slim indeed. Basically, my right hand serves as the swing's ignition key, ensuring that everything gets going correctly from the first split-second of motion.

I'm not a believer in singling out one segment of the golf swing and describing it in detail without showing its relationship to the entire action. So, for now, I'll describe only my concept of the correct takeaway, rather than its detailed mechanics.

Most instructors focus on left-hand or left-side dominance of the swing's initiation because they believe that, if a golfer activates his right hand early in the swing, he's liable to lift the club up too quickly, or jerk it too far to the inside of the target line, or otherwise distort either the path of the clubhead or the alignment of the clubface, or both.

I understand this reasoning, because, shortly after making the switch to right-hand control, I fell victim to both of these faults. Lifting the club straight up stunted my takeaway, and thereby restricted me from completely coiling my upper body. And, of course, coiling the body is the only way to pack power into the golf swing.

Jerking the club to the inside on too flat or shallow a path or plane required me to do some rerouting coming down in order to put everything back on track, which upset my rhythm. Eventually, I concluded that if I was going to permit my right hand to control the takeaway, the movement had to be a very deliberate one—indeed, slower than any other action in the swing. Finally, I sorted out the problem by learning to work my right hip "in

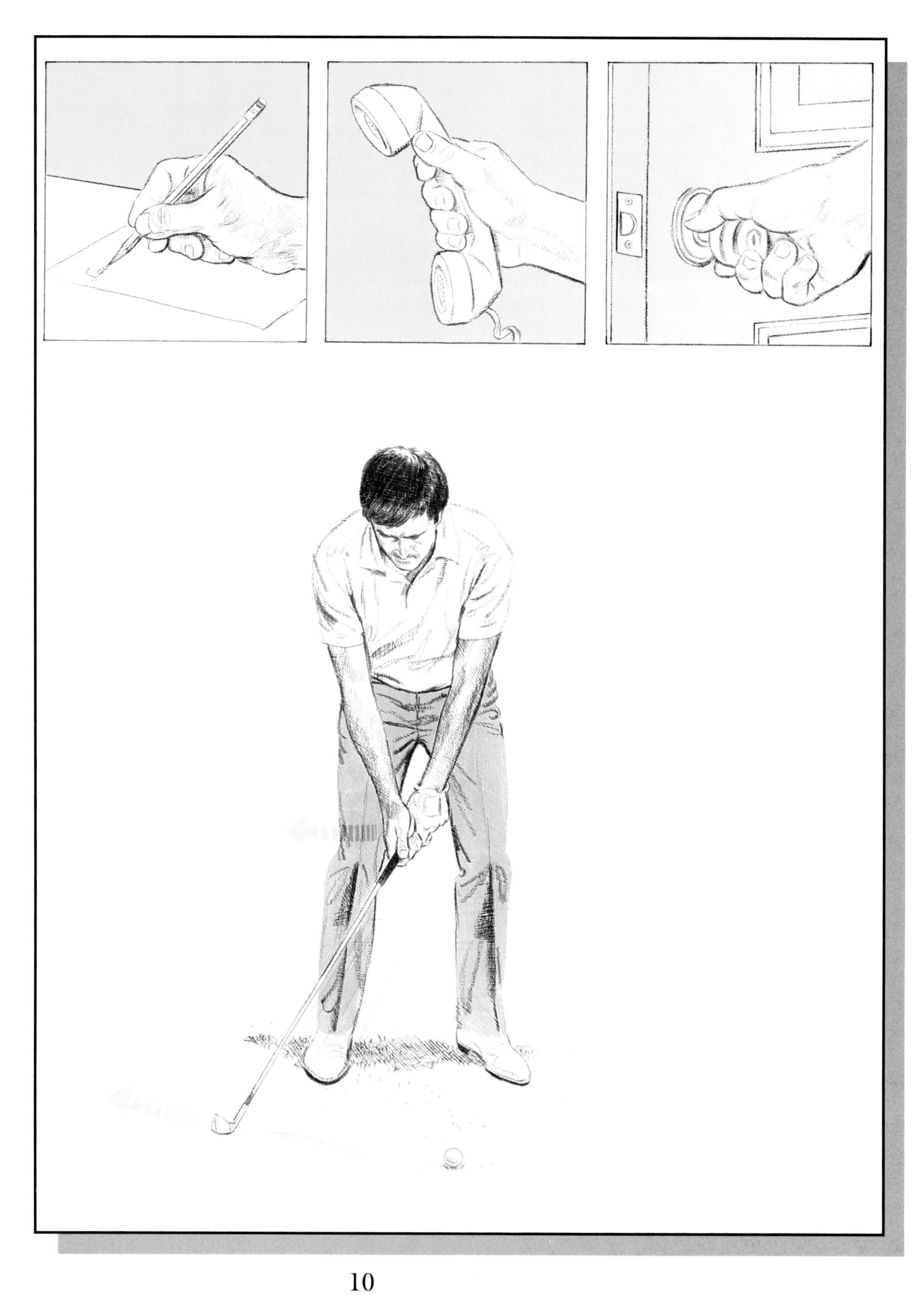

time" with the motion of my hands and the clubhead. In brief at this point, turning my right hip clockwise, an instant after I start pulling the club away from the ball *gently* with my right hand, sets off a most positive chain reaction in which my body coils smoothly and fully and my rhythm is excellent.

One footnote: I keep my wrists uncocked as I move the clubhead straight back from the ball and "quietly" along a rearward extension of the target line. Once the majority of my weight shifts to the inside of my right foot, I'm ready to cock my wrists and let the clubhead swing upward.

Using my strongest hand to start the swing enables me to better—i.e., more naturally and fluidly—control the pace of my takeaway; to pull the club away on the correct path; and to keep it traveling on the proper plane and arc. When my left hand was the ignition key, I had to think very hard all the time about what I was doing, and even then I found it difficult to achieve these three things because the action, being so contrary to my nature, felt so awkward. That threw off my timing and tempo, making it difficult to properly use the parts of my body that I depend on more than any other in swinging the club—my hands.

I don't want to go into too much more detail on this subject at this point for fear of confusing you, but I will say that, whenever I watch even the best left-sided players swing, it looks to me as though they are straining both mentally and physically—are being forced to think and work extra hard to keep the right hand "tame." Physically, they often appear to be actually holding back with their right side. To me this is a deadly sin, for in my case two major objectives of the takeaway are starting the weight moving to the right side and beginning the coiling of the upper and middle sections of the body in that direction. Right-hand control, along with the synchronization of the right-hip move that I've only just touched on, enables me most easily to achieve those goals.

Allowing my right hand to play a lively role in the swing is for me both natural and logical. After all, I've always depended on my right hand far more than my left for performing the activities of living.

Just before I start the swing, I often say to myself, "Right-hand takeaway"—that being my triggering key or cue. After that, however, the action is all about feel and muscle memory.

LISTENING TO ONE'S BODY

The question I'm asked the most by other golfers is: "Seve, were you born with your great 'feel'?" It never fails to bring a smile to my face, and I probably don't have to tell you why.

Before getting to work on this book, I'd never really thought too much about how to analyze and describe the feeling of the motion of the golf swing, but I suppose it can be compared to a person who suddenly has lost his sight learning to get around in a big city. He must determine the best way to grip his cane, how far to hold it out in front of him, the speed of stride that's easiest to control. He must find the best routes to travel and remember where he's probably going to run into trouble. Most of all, he must *listen intently* to what is going on all around him, as well as to his own footsteps.

In much the same manner, I "listen" very carefully to my body all the time as it swings the golf club. I want to know the role each part of me plays—what relationship my head, shoulders, arms, hands, hips, legs, and feet have to each other. I want particularly to know the sequence of their motion from start to finish.

For example, I told you my first move is to pull the club away from the ball gently, to drag the clubhead straight back and close to the ground for approximately the first foot of the swing. If this task is properly executed, I know that my arms will then swing easily and naturally for the remainder of the backswing, with the left shoulder moving nicely under my chin and my upper body gradually coiling like a spring, until it is tight-wound and ready to "snap" powerfully into the downswing. I want to know what each move feels like when it's correct—and what every possible fault anywhere along the way feels like, too. So, I am always looking to feel more and think less, both on the practice tee and on the course itself.

Sometimes, I want to grab and shake the golfer who is obviously thinking too much, the overintellectualizer forever geometrically analyzing his swing, stopping it at various points and checking and rechecking positions for "beauty"—as if he were trying on a suit and looking in a mirror from all angles. When I witness such a show I feel like yelling: "The golf swing is one continuous uninterrupted motion! You can't stop and start it like that!" I guess the reason I get irritated is because I see in this type of player a mirror image of the young and desperately searching—and extremely frustrated—Seve Ballesteros.

It took me many years to see the light. Anyone can find and "freeze" supposedly key swing positions when they're not actually trying to hit a golf ball. However, to do so is a complete waste of time, because the sole purpose of the golf swing is *to make square clubface-to-ball contact at speed*, and the only way to achieve that is *with flowing, controlled motion*. To repeat: It doesn't matter if you look like a beast before or after the hit, as long as you look like a beauty at the exact moment of impact.

Through frustration sometimes severe enough to put me in black depressions, I finally jettisoned all thoughts of trying to build what might be called an esthetically picture-perfect swing many years ago. What I began looking for were results, function, *effectiveness*. I believe I not only found these things personally but can, now, after that long and hard process, help others to do so. I believe my method is easier physically; takes less time to learn; will suit almost any golfer, weak or strong, high or low handicap; is long-lasting; and is more repeatable. And that final word is the ultimate key—repeatability. If anything is perfection in golf, that's it.

USE YOUR INTELLECT, TOO

A reasonable intellectual grasp of what you are trying to do with the golf club is important, too, because sometimes "feeling" the swing is a lot easier said than done. Many times I feel like I'm swinging smoothly and correctly, but the shots don't go where I want them to. This is when I turn to analyzing the ball's flight pattern, an invaluable aid to solving swing faults, and one that in my early youth enabled me to learn many new shots. Here's how that happened.

One day I was practicing full shots from a fairly good lie, flying ball after ball relatively straight. Then, out of the blue, the flight pattern changed to a fade, the ball curving slightly from left-to-right. I stopped to take inventory:

My finish: I was ending up with almost all of my weight on my right foot, instead of on the outside of my left foot. My divots: The fact that the divots pointed left of my target while the shots curved in the opposite direction puzzled me. My alignment: Allowing my upper and lower body to unravel back to the address position, I put a club across my toes, as I had seen Uncle Ramon do, then looked at the alignment from behind. From this vantage point, I could see that I had moved out of position, setting my body "open" or aligned to the left, rather than "square" or parallel to the target line.

I moved to another spot and carried the experiment a step further. With the ball played opposite my left heel, I took an open body alignment and set the club squarely behind the ball and facing dead at my target, then swung. The ball started left, then curved back to the right.

After a few more such shots, it all fell into place. Aiming my feet, hips, knees, and shoulders left caused me to swing the club away from my body, or outside the target line going back, and toward it and then across the line coming down. Cutting across the ball thus caused the divot to point left (where the ball started), and the shot to curve right, due to the sidespin I was imparting to it because the clubface was oblique—in this case, open to the path of the swing.

What an eyeopener that was! I had pinpointed my faults and, in so doing, taught myself how to hit a soft fade—at will.

This accidental learning experience prompted me to begin purposely altering my setup and ball position to see what effect the changes had on my swing path and the flight of the ball. In addition to the fade, I quickly learned how to hit the ball high, low, and from right-to-left (which is now my natural shape of shot), as well as becoming much better acquainted with the keys to power and accuracy, along with many of the elements that helped me to eventually develop a well-rounded short game.

"INVENTING" A SHORT GAME

If I had been formally taught the short game, I probably would have learned to hit the "basic" pitch shot and the "basic" chip shot and stopped there, so that my capabilities around the green would have been much less versatile. However, because I experimented so much—varying my setup and the length of my swing, aligning the clubface square, open, and closed, using different clubs, hitting different distances and from widely varying lies—I learned what most analysts of the game regard as a commanding arsenal of recovery shots.

To help me learn hand-eye coordination, and the fine points of spin, I noted very carefully how the ball reacted to each switch in lie and technique. To help me stay sharp, I played little games in practice, pretending on each shot that I had to get the ball within tap-in range to win a major championship. Today, I really believe that such youthful fantasizing helped train me to handle the enormous competitive pressures that came later.

This "preparation"—and it always comes back to that—helped me to develop what it takes to get the ball close to the pin and then down in one putt from all over the place: To get "up and down" as the pros say, to roll three shots into two and two into one, which, in the final analysis, is the *real* difference between being a four-star general and a buck private on today's world tournament scene.

Maybe the best single example of how this early training helped took place in the 1976 British Open at Royal Birkdale. In my travels it seems the whole world saw me there on television, but, in case you didn't, let me say that this was the occasion when, at age nineteen, I made my first real mark on the golfing public and press, not least by hitting what still remains one of my most memorable shots.

The final hole at Royal Birkdale is a 536-yard par-five. My second shot in the last round finished pin-high to the left of the green, 25 yards from the flag, in threadbare rough trampled down all week by the huge galleries. In front of me were two bunkers guarding a fast-running green baked bone dry by the sun and wind.

Most players who have been taught golf formally would have visualized, and attempted, some kind of pitch shot over the bunkers. To me, such a strategy offered no percentage, especially with the wind at my back. There was a one-in-a-hundred, maybe a one-in-a-thousand, chance to loft the ball cleanly off the dry ground and have it land on the firm putting surface with enough "bite" to stop close to the hole. First off, the pitching-wedge does not have enough loft to achieve such superspin. Second, the ground was so hard that the sand-wedge, with its flanged sole, would have bounced off it, probably causing a "skulled" or topped shot. Third, because of the short distance, I couldn't hit the ball firmly enough to impart much backspin.

I knew the shot to play, and I mentally pictured it immediately. It was a pitch-and-run up a narrow grass path running between the bunkers. I visualized the ball landing in the middle of the path, bouncing once, and rolling toward the pin.

Selecting a 9-iron, I took an open stance, giving me a clear picture of the route, and checked that my left arm and clubshaft formed a straight line. I set my weight left and kept it there, since this shot calls for no shifting of the weight or coiling of the body, and only a slight rotation of the knees. I set the clubface square to the target and kept my eyes on the back of the ball, which I had positioned well back in my stance. Then, gripping a hair more firmly with my left hand, I made a one-piece takeaway, swinging the straight line formed by my left arm and clubshaft back together, with no wrist cock. I made only a short backswing, about a one-quarter motion up to knee height, then swung firmly back down again, gently accelerating the blade through the ball.

The shot came off exactly as I'd visualized it, the ball finishing four feet from the hole, close enough for me to make the birdie and tie Jack Nicklaus for second place behind Johnny Miller. "Miraculous," the press called it. They wondered how such a young and inexperienced player could pull off such a stroke at such a time. Some of the writers deemed me a "shotmaking genius."

What many of them failed to realize is that I was *not* inexperienced. I had spent eleven years prior to that championship learning to hit a very wide variety of golf shots, including the one I called upon on that final hole at Royal Birkdale.

Without that early self-education, I would have been an average student with a limited imagination, and that chip heard around the world would never have come to mind.

And that, my friends, is the payoff for teaching yourself how to play this wonderful game.

Chapter 2

HOW I LEARNED TO PLAY GOLF

Many of my family and friends credit my success to *destino*, the Spanish word for destiny. To tell you the truth, I'm tired of hearing such talk, because, even during my childhood, I believed destiny to be much more a matter of choice than chance.

In my mind, no golfer has ever been "destined" to become a fine player. The willingness—or, better yet, the eagerness, or better even yet, the *compulsion*—to work continuously at building and preserving an all-around sound game may be a matter of genetic luck. Beyond that, it all comes down to practice and perseverance. To be sure, some of you will find golf harder to play well than others, for any one of a number of reasons. Nevertheless, if you keep studying and working, you *will* improve, and the more you do the more enjoyment and satisfaction you will get from the game.

Early on, I realized that *destino*, although a nice idea, wasn't really in the cards, and that it was either the hard road or no road at all for Seve Ballesteros as far as golf was concerned. A lot of people in similar circumstances might have thrown in the towel, but quitting has never been in my nature. If fate couldn't achieve what I wanted, I decided that sheer fortitude could—and would.

This attitude stopped me from feeling sorry for myself, but, much more important than that, it shaped my entire future. Every day that I practiced—and I practiced every day, without fail—I became more and more fired up by the sheer scale of the effort I was making to become the greatest golfer in the world. Very soon, I had come to believe that nothing—but *nothing*—could stop me from achieving that goal.

It made no difference that our family's modest farming income forced me to make do in many ways, as for instance in learning with only one club, first with the 3-iron I've mentioned, then with a 5-iron after my "old faithful" was stolen, while the sons of wealthy club members showed off their sparkling new matched sets. It still sometimes burns me to think that, in 1965, while I was an eight year old hacking away in the fields of Pedreña, many of my American contemporaries were receiving top-grade formal instruction and playing regularly on the finest championship courses. The reason is, of course, that back then golf was very small beer indeed in Spain. There were no golf magazines, and no telecasts of even the top tournaments. Sportswriters focused almost entirely on soccer superstars, and TV sports show ratings only rose when a bull was shown mauling a matador. I had to borrow shoes from the locker room man at Pedreña, and beg a member to lend me his set of clubs, so I could play in the annual caddie championship.

The odds were surely against me, but the higher they mounted the greater became my will to overcome. "Seve, one day you'll show them," a small but very clear voice inside my head kept telling me.

Deep down, I probably realized that learning to play golf with one club was a "poor man's method" of picking up the game, but I possessed far too much pride ever to admit that. By choosing instead to dream always of success, I was able to convince myself that this unique apprenticeship would, one day, make me incomparably rich in shotmaking skills.

From time to time I dwell on my past, and I wonder what life would have been like had I come from less humble circumstances. Each time, I come to the same conclusions.

I suspect my formative golfing days would have been more "gentlemanly," and certainly easier materially, but they also would have been less exciting. As a youngster, I probably would have taken regular lessons from a good teacher each summer, and soon played to a low handicap at the local country club. However, in such circumstances I just cannot imagine myself ever inventing shots with a 3-iron, and in that respect there is absolutely no question in my mind that I would have been a lesser golfer today.

By the same token, had the Spanish Golf Federation seen fit to make provisions for juniors of nongolfing parents to play their local courses, I'm sure I would not have been inspired to construct a little golf course in the fields near our small farm. As it was, my love for the game was so great that I spent days pulling up weeds and shoveling and stamping down dirt to make two more-or-less level tees and greens, then setting tomato cans for cups and sticks cut from the woods for flags on both the 100-yard and 180-yard holes I built.

In addition to playing my two-hole "St. Andrews," I practiced on the nearby beach in solitude day after day for hour after hour, or snuck on the local course with my friends, either at dawn or just before darkness set in over Pedreña. And, again, what many would regard as a handicap turned out to be a benefit by continually strengthening my resolve to master the game, whatever the cost.

Practicing alone helped me to come to terms with golf's most important commandments, which are that this is first a game of Man against Himself, and next a game of Man against Course, and it also taught me a lot about patience. Hitting shots with friends and betting on the outcome sharpened my competitive spirit, while priming me in the handling of competitive pressure. Putting in near darkness taught me much that otherwise I might never have learned about the stroke: The line to the hole was so dim that I was forced to concentrate on keeping my head quiet and my body perfectly still, and on making a smooth low-back-and-through motion with the putter blade.

Sadly, even today in Spain—and I'm sure in other countries—catering to wealthy club members takes precedence over providing opportunities for less fortunate juniors to learn and play golf. I keep hoping my wins around the world will inspire my country's golfing leaders to modernize their thinking and change the old policies, but progress is very slow. Yet the situation is at least a little better than when I was growing up—or even in 1978, when I won my first U.S. PGA Tour tournament, the Greater Greensboro Open.

Greensboro is played a week prior to the Masters Tournament, and I naturally thought my victory there—the first by a Spaniard in the U.S.—would spark so much attention that the Spanish sportswriters would flock to Augusta to watch me play in the first of the year's major championships. Boy, am I glad I didn't hold my breath for that one! Believe it or not, the only thing that happened is that one paper called to say that, if I dictated a brief daily report by phone, it would "try" to print the story. That presents an interesting picture, doesn't it? I'm sure you can just see me standing in a phone booth in Augusta, Georgia, calling in Masters scores to Spain.

Unfortunately, such memories don't stop with Augusta that year. Shortly after winning my second British Open Championship at St. Andrews in 1984, I tried to convince the local mayor to have a public golf course constructed. At the beginning of 1988 there still was no sign of it happening.

On the positive side, there's some talk of school teams and scholarship funds being set up, so that maybe one day Spanish professionals will emerge from colleges as well as caddie yards. Furthermore, with golf purses growing to ever more gigantic proportions, perhaps even the sons and daughters of the affluent and socially prominent will be allowed to pursue golf as a profession, rather than shooting for the standard law degree or seat on the stock exchange.

CONCENTRATION—MY STRONGEST SUIT

If I sound like a salesman for learning golf with one club, that's because I'm convinced that this type of practice encourages you to work your body and the club in so many different ways that using your imaginative powers in later years to invent shots becomes virtually second nature. Playing with one club also inspires you to consider more carefully the lie of the land you're hitting to, in order to make the *next* shot as easy as possible, due to the much smaller margin for error involved when every stroke must be "manufactured" in a different way both mentally and physically.

Ever since boyhood, when often I felt as if I lived in a cocoonlike state inside some kind of "bubble," concentration has been a strong part of my game. Nowadays, I enter the bubble as early as three weeks prior to each of golf's four major championships. Like clockwork, a cloud comes over me and grows ever denser as these critical events draw nearer. In this state, I'm so busy psyching and pumping myself up to play winning golf that people seem to be talking to me through a pane of glass. It's a strange sensation: I can hear them all right, but their voices are muted.

By the time the tournament arrives, I'm so deeply immersed in my game plan and my play that I'm virtually oblivious to outside sights and sounds. For instance, I never hear my playing partner's clubs rattling, and I rarely ever hear the gallery applauding. Even after the round, when I return to my hotel room, all hell could break loose and I would never know it. I'm in a world of my own.

So, if you happen to see me with a very serious or even a stern or frowning look on my face during the Masters, U.S. Open, British Open, or PGA Championship, don't think badly of me. I assure you, when I wear the face of an iceman, it just means that I'm grinding as hard as I can inside my bubble to win the championship.

The first time I was able to fully envelop myself in the cocoon since childhood was during the 1979 British Open at Royal Lytham & St. Anne's. I won that championship, but the feeling of isolated concentration I experienced during it frightened me so much that I looked for a professional explanation of it. A doctor friend of mine told me that the young and supercompetitive Seve Ballesteros—*who had to make it at all costs*—simply was reincarnated around major championship time. When I retreated into the bubble, I was literally back in my adolescence.

I had better clarify this. It doesn't mean I'm some kind of Jekyll-and-Hyde personality. Hopefully, I'm the same adult and mature and reasonably well-balanced Seve Ballesteros most of the time. However, the solitary boy, who closed himself off so completely from the outside world so that he could truly give his "all" to golf, is still a very strong part of me, and under certain competitive conditions that part takes over. And I'm thankful this is so, because of its beneficial effects on all aspects of my game.

The major championships are extremely emotional tests for me, so much so that I'm in a state of high mental tension from the time I hit my first tee shot to the moment I sink my final putt. Maybe this is why I weep happy tears when I win and cry sad tears when I lose.

Reading this, you might think the majors are all that matter to me. That's not so, because I am simply too competitive not to try to win every time I tee it up. However, to put the "majors" versus "the rest" comparison into true perspective, let me just say: I prefer to eat salmon, but I enjoy also trout.

THE ROCKY ROAD OF A DETERMINED YOUTH

Obviously, from what I've just explained, the chief reason I play hard all the time, and even harder some of the time, is the very deep sense of determination I developed in my youth.

On most summer days, I started my practice sessions shortly after sunup, and, even when I broke for a snack, would drop my soup spoon and run the second some new swing thought came to mind. Writing it down as quickly as I could, I would race out the door, totally incapable of waiting to test out my new theory. "Seve, where are you going? Are you crazy?" my mother would yell after me, time and time again. And I was, indeed, just that —totally crazy about golf.

As I've said, I depended almost solely on my instinctive and imaginative powers to guide me, and, because I was literally the producer, director, and lead actor in my "play," there were some pretty rough passages along the way.

Right off the bat, I fell victim to the "macho" syndrome, trying foolishly to hit every shot as hard as I possibly could. Boy, if I only knew then what I know now about the secret to powerful hitting! Plain and simple, clubhead speed is *not* the only answer to distance in golf, whatever you may have heard or read to that effect. Rather, the key is to swing at a speed that enables you to *repeatedly strike the ball squarely with the sweetspot of the clubface.*

(A few years ago, I confirmed this to myself while testing a new computerized swing machine at the Tournament Players Club in Florida. When sticking to my normal tempo, my body and the club worked as a cohesive and efficient team, producing drives, according to the computer readout, consistently of about 250 yards. In contrast, when I really let rip, invariably I mistimed the action and, even though I generated about 20 mph more clubhead speed—140 rather than 120 mph—the computer indicated that I carried the ball 10 yards less on average.)

Without meaning to sound cocky or big-headed, I think that my swing tempo, when I am playing at my best, is the finest in the business. But, believe me, getting to that point was a long haul. The basic reason was what I think of as gaps, or power leaks, in my action.

Viewing old photographs of my swing, I sometimes look to myself like a crazed marionette, all wild and loose and disjointed, especially in the wrists, with a lot of unnecessary body twisting and turning on the way back and slipping and sliding on the way down. Instead of making one continuous and controlled flowing motion—as every golfer must learn to do if he wants to achieve square and speedy contact—I swung the club way beyond the parallel position at the top, then, coming down, put literally every ounce of strength I possessed into trying to knock the cover off the ball. It was the granddaddy of overswings, and, for every shot I hit solidly down the middle, three flew wildly, which wasn't too good a percentage for a guy who had decided to become the world's finest golfer.

The beginning of the change came from losing all of my golf balls in the woods one day. Not wanting to go home for fear of being put to work on the family farm, I started trying some

To me, being in the comfort zone means entering a "bubble" of intense concentration—a place to temper my will and gather my thoughts and plan strategies and shots with no outside interference.

"silly" swings. I made a pass with my right hand only, then with my left alone, then knelt down and swung, then kept my feet together, then stood on my left foot only—each time taking a swat at an imaginary ball. To say that these exercises worked a miracle would be an exaggeration. What they did do was help me, for the first time, to begin to truly "feel" the correct way to swing a golf club.

The left-hand-only swing told me that the left hand and arm are extensions of the club itself, and that this line must not alter significantly going back or break down at all at impact. I discovered that the takeaway was best controlled with my right hand, which later in the action served as a major power source. Kneeling down and swinging allowed me to instantly understand the importance of an upper body coil in the backswing. Swinging with my feet together impressed upon me the significance of a free-flowing arm swing. Swinging with only my left foot on the ground taught me the importance of shifting weight over to the left side on the downswing.

As I worked more and more on these drills, and thereby gradually came to incorporate each new element into my overall action, I found myself hitting the ball both a "little" more powerfully *and* a "little" more accurately. In short, my swing was getting closer to functioning as one cohesive unit. And yet, something was still missing. I knew this for sure, but, with no teacher to turn to, couldn't put my finger on it until several months later, when I discovered the elusive links in a better grip and setup. And, of course, we'll be examining those highly critical preswing factors in full detail later in the book.

DISCOVERING THOSE SHORT-GAME SECRETS

During that time I remember becoming particularly frustrated with not being able to get the ball home on Pedreña's "La Riviera" 198-yard hole, and thus finally taking my brother Manuel's long-proffered advice: "Seve, go learn how to get the ball up and down . . . then you can deal with all kinds of trouble."

This time, instead of traveling the road alone, I got some help from four of my caddie friends, Juan, Jorge, José, and Salvador. And, although there's no doubt I taught myself most of what I know about golf, practicing with my *amigos* really helped me.

Because none of us had any formal tutoring, and therefore no real concept of golf's fundamentals, our setup positions constantly changed, which produced some pretty inventive swings. However, because the short game permits so much more versatility than the long game does, this served to our advantage.

There we were, the five of us, sharing my 3-iron and practicing either in the fields, or, when we could get away with it, surreptitiously on the Pedreña course, taking turns picking lies and hitting shots, and constantly learning from each others' successes and failures.

To my amazement, I quickly found the challenge of planning and playing a tricky recovery shot almost as exciting as trying to tear the cover off the ball. I guess that was because, after fluffing and skulling a few such shots, I came to realize and accept that,

Making "silly swings" during my youth led me to discover vital technical keys—among them that the right hand ideally controls the takeaway and later on becomes a major source of power.

to become a short-game wizard, you need to depend much more on "mind" than on "muscle"—much more on imagination and touch than on strength and mechanics.

I still remember seeing the ball fly faster off the clubface when wet grass intervened between the two, or from a perched lie, and wondering how I was ever going to learn how to control such a shot. Then, gradually, by trial and error, I eventually discovered the best way to handle these "flyer" lies: Swinging on an out-to-in path allows you to cut across the ball through impact, thereby imparting left-to-right sidespin, which automatically flies the ball higher and takes some of the "heat" off the shot.

The same patient, step-by-step process taught me how to hit a short shot softly, even when the ball sat snugly in heavy rough. I found that opening the blade, swinging back at a steep angle, dropping the clubhead easily into the grass behind the ball, and keeping most of the weight on the right side in the hitting area makes the ball pop out "quietly."

If I'm making it sound as though there is just one solution for every on-course problem, I'm leading you astray. And that was another bonus of learning with my friends. Often, each of us would use totally different techniques and yet still get the ball close to the hole.

Observing that phenomenon eventually opened up a whole new world for me. In addition to discovering that there were various ways to the same end, it occurred to me that, the more techniques you equip yourself with, the more imaginative you become—and the more imaginative you become the more recovery techniques you then continue manufacturing. The result today is that, during a seventy-two-hole tournament, although I may face a similar lie four days running, I will rarely play the same shot twice from it.

THE VALUE OF A VIVID IMAGINATION

Unlike the formally schooled "mechanical" player who has been taught essentially one basic swing, and therefore tends to "see" only one basic kind of golf shot, I can swing the club effectively in a wide variety of ways, and in consequence am able to visualize several shots in pretty much any situation. And, of course, it is the imaginative powers developed through learning the game essentially with one club that underlie this tremendous competitive weapon.

Even though I may never have played a particular shot with a particular club, I can make a pretty good guess at what the ball will do, both in the air and on the ground, simply because I have imagined and then played so many different kinds of shots with one club. The sensation is a lot like hearing a new song, and being able to predict where the music is going to go, just because you have heard such a variety of tunes before.

One-club practice trains you to be able to choose from a whole arsenal of shots every time you get up to the ball. Then, by visualizing how high or low the ball will fly, how much and what kind of spin will be imparted to it, where it will land and how fast and far it will roll, you can weed out the shots that won't work, leaving yourself ultimately with the *ideal* shot for just about any given situation.

To my mind, clearly seeing such galaxies of shots in one's mind's eye, and being able to predict the outcome of each, is what true golfing "feel" is all about. And, of course, being able then to execute each of them as called upon is the ultimate form of percentage golf.

The greatest secret to learning golf with one club is letting your imagination truly run wild. Set the ball "up" and "down" in the grass. Take square, open, and closed stances. Play the ball well forward, way back, and everywhere in between. Swing on an upright plane and on a flat plane. Swing with active hands and passive hands. Put some leg drive into the shot one time, leave it out the next. Move the club on an out-to-in and an in-to-out path. Hit long shots, then middle-distance shots, then short shots, with the same club. Go with your instincts, all the time carefully watching and feeling which actions do what to the ball, then memorizing and learning from them.

Although it was my first club—by happenstance, not choice—I know now that the 3-iron was far from being the best learning tool. Because of the club's lack of loft, the ball often shot off the

The 7-iron is the ideal club for ingraining good technique and a fine sense of touch. This club's comparatively short shaft and upright lie promote a controlled swinging action on the proper plane. Furthermore, the 7-iron's thirty-nine degrees of loft induces confidence about easily getting the ball well up into the air.

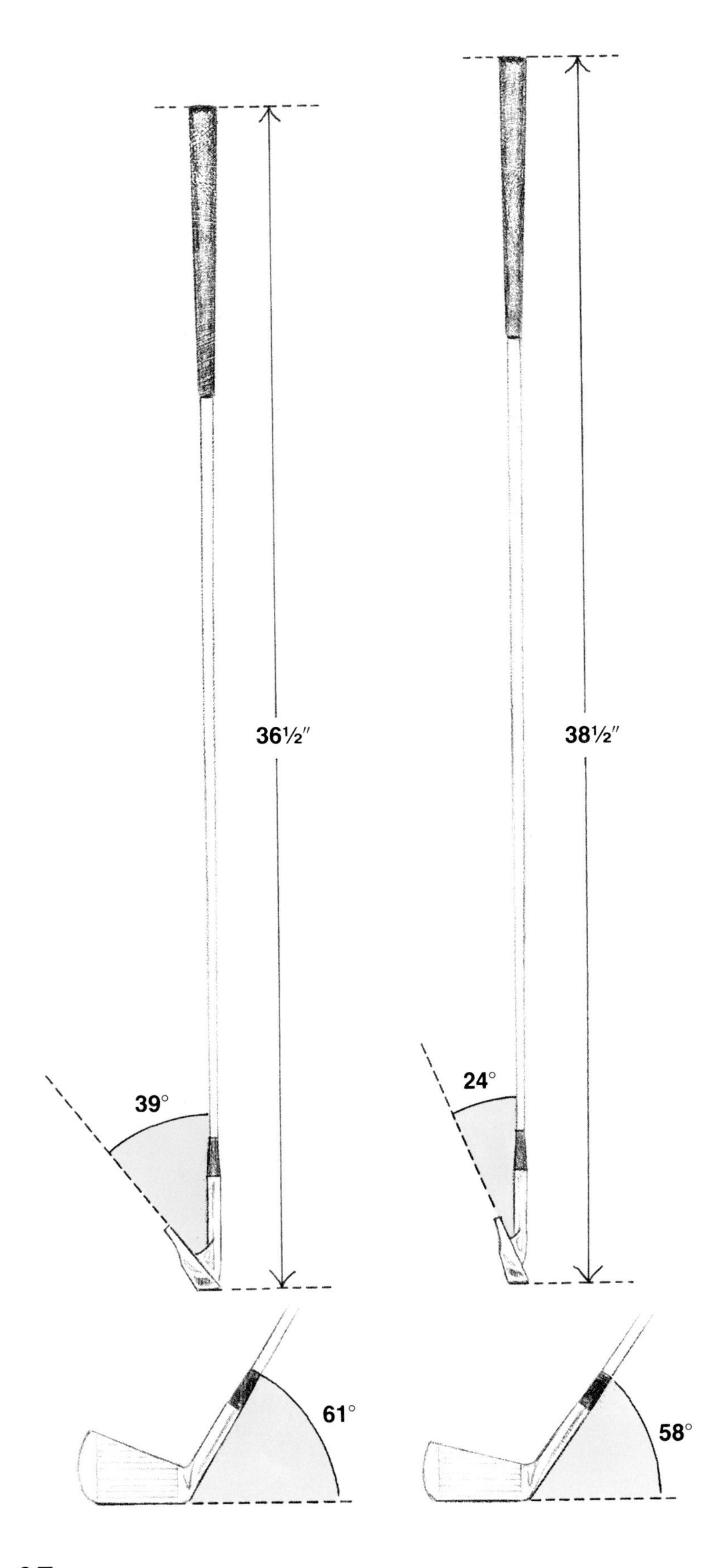

face "hot," so I had to drastically exaggerate and work excessively hard to hit many of the short finesse shots I needed or wanted to play, especially those calling for height or a soft landing.

However, there was a positive side to this predicament that definitely contributed to my reaching my present stage as a shotmaker. By having to magnify every move of my body and the club, each key action was deeply impressed in my mind. Also, the experience taught me how to work the club in all sorts of ways almost entirely with my hands.

I've decided that, if I had it all to do over again, my choice of club would be the 7-iron. The reason is that the 7-iron is the club I consider the perfect learning tool for developing the keenest possible sense of touch.

The 7-iron has, at thirty-nine degrees of loft, fifteen more than the 3-iron; is two inches shorter in the shaft; and, most importantly, it is more upright in lie and therefore far less cumbersome to swing. Coping with the 3-iron's longer shaft and flatter lie was a real hurdle for me, particularly in my younger and smaller days. I always felt I had to get out of the way of the long shaft, so I swayed off the ball with my body, which made me swing the club too much around my back, causing a swing plane that was for some years too flat. (Although this isn't the place to go deeply into this aspect of the swing, I will tell you that I am not a believer in a flat swing for anyone other than a very short person, whose only way to generate a good body coil is by making a very rounded action.)

Because of its relatively short shaft and upright lie, you will instinctively groove a more upright swing path by learning the game with the 7-iron. I see this as a major benefit, not only because an upright swing is ideal for playing most short shots, but also because the laws of physics dictate that this pattern of swing gives the golfer his best chance of delivering the clubhead directly along the target line through impact, for the simple reason that the club moves less far off that line during the action than it does during a flat swing.

So, if you decide to give the one-club method a try, be sure above all to work on hitting as many different shots as you can imagine. Give it a little time and I think you will be very pleasantly surprised at how much it helps *every* aspect of your golf game.

IMAGINATION—THE MOTHER OF INVENTION

I approach my one-club practice sessions in the same way a pianist sits down to improvise a melody. He lets his mind and fingers wander freely, hitting keys at random, until he feels he's on to something good.

Just following my instincts, I constantly change my setup, while swinging the club along different paths and planes, searching for new shots that will save me strokes.

Unfortunately, the typical club golfer rarely does any experimental practice, usually because he seeks basically one standard swing, which he feels he needs to work on unrelentingly for fear of having "nothing to play with" on the golf course.

I respect a systematic approach. On the other hand, I feel strongly that there is a negative side to sticking to a regimented practice routine in that you never give yourself the chance to find a better way to play a particular shot—in short, to improve.

During rest periods in Santander, when I'm far away from the pressure of tournament golf, I continually look for new approaches to shotmaking. Then, I'm not afraid to try *anything*. And it is this open-minded attitude that allowed me to recently learn a new sand shot. Let me share it with you.

In the past, I'd been unable to consistently get the ball close to the cup when it was sitting cleanly but tight to a high lip with the hole cut close to the edge of the bunker's wall. The solution I stumbled on through experimentation is essentially to choke down on the sand-wedge so that my "control" hand grips the steel shaft of the club.

This simple maneuver encourages breaking the wrists very early in the takeaway, and thus swinging the club up and down at a particularly steep angle. Equally importantly, your hand speed quickens automatically, as the thin shaft slides through your fingers—a move that allows the club to more easily "scalp" the sand and slip beneath the ball. Result: The ball floats up over the lip, lands softly, and stops quickly.

Now, to try to convince you, once and for all, that there *are* alternatives to regimented or one-system practice and that they work wonders, let me tell you how I learned this technique.

I had cut down an old 7-iron and a sand-wedge for my brother Manuel's young son, Sergio, to practice with. During our "play," I decided, using Sergio's new short-shafted sand-wedge, to show him how to recover from bunkers. Kids are great at copying, so I asked him only to watch my technique closely. After effortlessly splashing a few shots dead to the pin, then a few shots with my own sand-wedge choking way down, I knew I had made a big discovery.

It confirmed my belief that every golfer has the capacity to invent shots that may work better for him than the textbook solutions—once he trusts himself enough to break away and do his own experimentation.

Experimental practice can teach you valuable new shots, like this one I learned. When the ball is sitting cleanly in a bunker, but uncomfortably close to its lip, choking well down on the sand-wedge encourages you to swing back at the proper steep angle, then "scalp" the sand perfectly with the club as you slip it beneath the ball. The result is a shot that floats softly up over the lip and lands close to the hole with lots of "stop."

PART 2

THE BIG SWINGS

Chapter 3

HOLDING RIGHT

Instinctively, I've always swung the club predominantly with my hands, probably because I was blessed with big, strong ones. Had I been formally taught golf, I probably would have learned to swing more with my arms or body, which I'm sure would have led me to develop a stiffer, more mechanical action. If that had happened, I doubt if I would have achieved the finely tuned feel for the clubhead that is the chief reason I am able to play such a wide variety of golf shots today.

I control the club with a gentle pulling action of the hands on the backswing, then an almost entirely reflexive but slightly more powerful reciprocal pulling action in the downswing. I believe strongly that this is the most logical approach to swinging, simply because it makes sense to give the only parts of the body directly connected to the golf club the chief role in controlling it. However, none of us should lose sight of the fact that a precise and powerful golf swing depends on an effective sequential action and reaction of the entire body. That means that trying to swing the club solely with the hands isn't the answer, any more than swinging with the body so drastically that the hands are largely taken out of the swing is the answer.

After making those two discoveries by painful trial and error at a fairly early age, I began to search for a simple key that would allow me to establish the proper balance between dead and overlively hands, while at the same time bringing my arms and body correctly into play once I had triggered the swing. Eventually, I discovered the key in a correct grip.

All golfers who, like me, feel they hit the ball "with" rather than "through" the hands are inclined to rate the grip as the guts of the swing. That's because of the numerous good things a well-molded grip allows you to achieve in return for a fairly simple and easily ingrained procedure. These are:

1. Align the clubface squarely to the target as you stand to the ball readying yourself to swing.

2. Start the swing correctly with a low-to-the-ground sweep of the clubhead directly back along the target line.

3. Hold onto the club with sufficient security to fully control it throughout the swing, most particularly at the top when the momentum of the clubhead puts heavy stress on the hands and wrists, and also at impact when the most powerful forces are being exerted.

4. Swing in good tempo by promoting proper balance between hand, wrist, arm, and body movement.

5. Efficiently transfer the power generated by the body to the clubhead.

6. Repeatedly return the clubface squarely to the ball traveling at speeds in excess of a hundred miles per hour, or the fastest your strength allows you to swing it in a controlled fashion.

Some amateurs fail to develop a good hold on the club due to sheer ignorance of the grip's importance. Others realize its crucial part in the game, but only in moments of utter desperation or high inspiration do they try to turn their bad grip into a good one, usually reverting as soon as they realize they aren't going to instantly become the next Arnold Palmer. Most just go along with what they sense or know to be a lousy grip out of sheer inertia, while perhaps harboring a vague hope that their swing will somehow sort itself out anyway. Unfortunately, it never will.

There is no guarantee that a newly corrected grip will suddenly fix a poor swing, and certainly not in a couple of practice sessions. In most cases, as in mine years ago, a golfer who makes the switch will swing the club pretty much the same way he's been accustomed to, at least during the initial stages of the transition, if only because swing faults caused by a flawed grip become so deeply ingrained and hard to break. Nevertheless, the payoff for persistence, patience, and practice in this area will be handsome indeed. And, of course, there is no option for any bad gripper truly determined to reach his full golfing potential but to earn that payoff.

Here's an exercise that will help you master the key fundamental of correctly setting both hands on the club. Imagine an iron club soled on the ground with its horizontal face grooves dead square to both the ball and the target. Next, stand to the imaginary club with your feet, knees, hips, and shoulders parallel to an imaginary line that runs directly from ball to target, while allowing your arms to hang naturally at your sides so that the palms of both hands face each other. Now, extend your arms and take the squarely aimed club in your hands *without changing the alignment of your palms.* This "palms-parallel" positioning is vital, because, once the swing is triggered, the hands *must* work largely as a single unit throughout the motion, which they will only do when their alignment matches.

Here are the other basics of a fine golf grip.

THE LEFT-HAND HOLD

You will achieve maximum grip security, without loss of feel or wrist flexibility, when you set the club's handle diagonally across the base of the fingers and partially in the palm of the left hand, with the butt end of it resting securely just below the heel pad.

To increase control over the club, allow your thumb to stretch straight down the shaft as far as comfortably possible (rather than letting it curl up with its tip riding down the right side of the shaft), thereby closing any gap between the palm and fingertips that might cause you to loosen your hold. Next, check that the back of the hand faces the target, and that between two and two and a half knuckles are visible to you when the clubface is set squarely behind the ball.

THE RIGHT-HAND HOLD

There are three variations on the way the right hand can be linked with the left on the handle of the club. Whichever you find most effective, you should form the right-hand grip as follows.

Set the club in the roots of the fingers, thereby giving the hand and wrist the free range of motion necessary to accelerate the clubhead to maximum speed through impact. As you close the right hand, be sure that the thumb pad covers your left thumb; that the palm faces the left palm; and that the thumb rides easily just to the left of the top of the shaft and pinches the tip of the right forefinger. Working the tips of the thumb and forefinger together activates the muscles in your right hand and arm, thereby encouraging the proper right-sided trigger action in the takeaway. At this point, all the fingers of the right and left hands are directly in contact with the club handle.

That's golf's most basic hold—the *ten-finger* or "baseball" grip, as it is commonly referred to in the U.S. One or two PGA Tour players with small or weaker hands use it, but most prefer to further unify the action of the hands by tying them even closer together. One way of doing that is by *interlocking*, the choice of Gene Sarazen and Jack Nicklaus, among others. To interlock, simply entwine your right pinky between the first and middle fingers of your left hand.

The most common form of hand "marrying" is the *overlap* grip, popularized by one of the game's first superstars, Harry Vardon, and favored ever since by the majority of golf's top players. Overlapping involves simply laying the right pinky over the top of the left forefinger, or—as I do for extra security and unity—letting it rest practically between the first and middle digits of the left hand.

Being a born experimenter, I've tried all three of these variations, but, even before turning professional, I decided on the overlap for several reasons.

A sound grip is the only way to consistently deliver the clubface squarely to the ball at high speed which is *the* "secret" to the game of golf.

The "palms-parallel" position is paramount to gripping correctly, which in turn is critical to swinging the club on the proper path and plane.

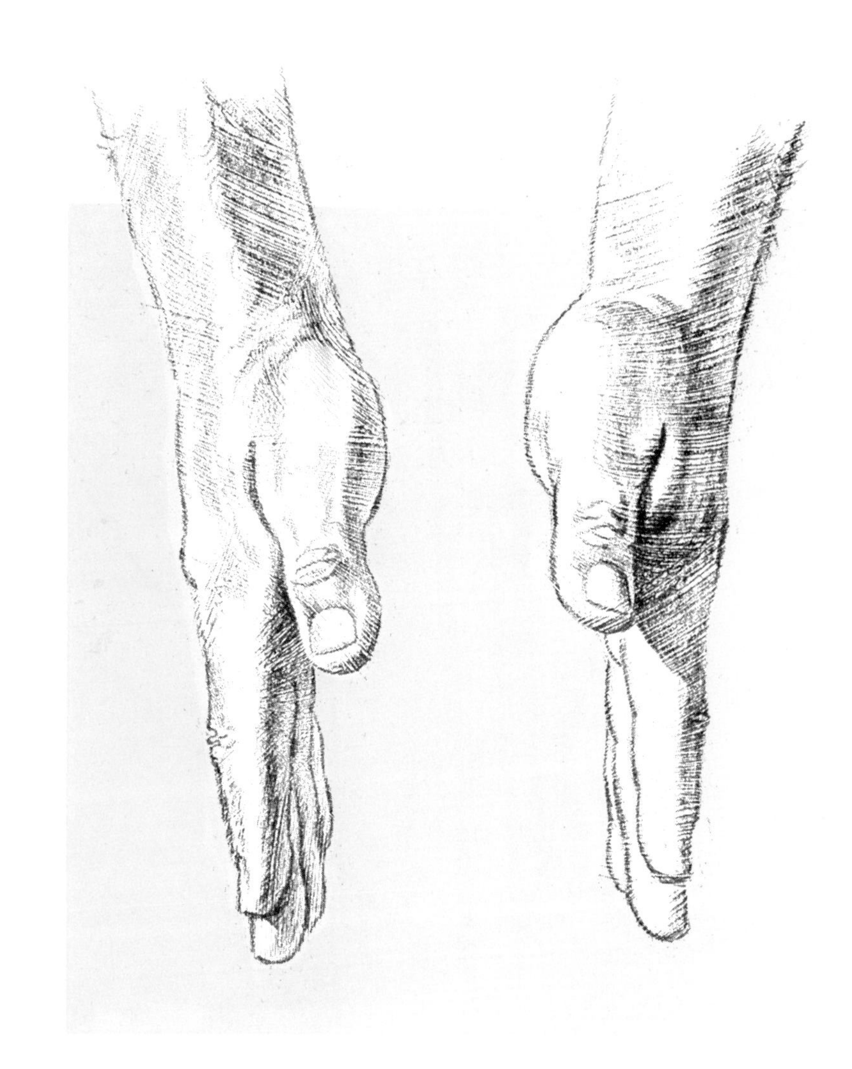

To maintain maximum control over the clubhead throughout the swing, I "connect" my hands to the club in a very particular way. Key points are that my left thumb is stretched straight down the shaft as far as it will comfortably go; that the back of my left hand is square to my target; and that the little finger of my right hand rides virtually piggyback atop the forefinger of my left hand.

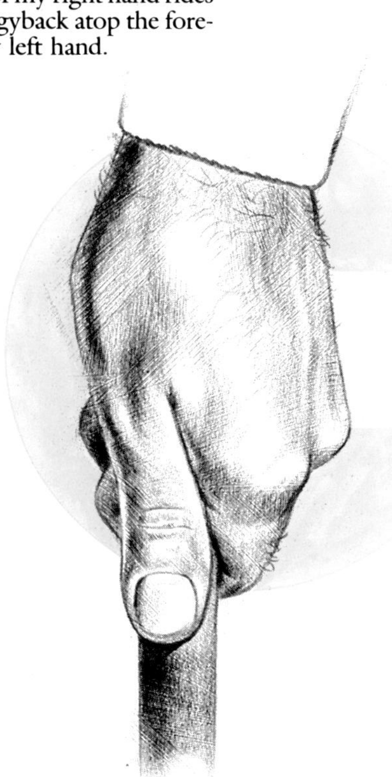

Obtaining the correct grip is a very personal process, thus you should experiment intelligently to find your ideal hold. For me, setting the hands in a "neutral" position—i.e., with the "V"s of each hand pointing pretty much midway between my chin and right shoulder—makes for consistently square and solid striking of the ball.

First, overlapping gives me a great feeling of instant unity in the hands, so that I am rarely inclined to fiddle with my fingers at address and thus seldom inadvertently move the clubhead into a faulty alignment once I've set its face squarely to the ball and my target.

Second, the overlap grip promotes a strong sense of security in my hands and wrists, while best allowing me to maintain a straight-line relationship with my left arm and the clubshaft as I start the swing. We've said before, and will stress again later, that this is critical to accurate and solid ball striking.

Third, the overlap or Vardon grip fits perfectly with my preference for right-hand control, allowing me to make the complex movements of the swing with relative consistency. Why? When my right pinky essentially rides piggyback on my left forefinger, rather than directly gripping the club, enough "muscle" is removed from my naturally stronger right hand to prevent it from overpowering my left, while still leaving the right in command because it sits closer to the clubhead than the left.

In toying with the interlock grip, my hands "looked" more unified because the right pinky wrapped itself so snugly around the left forefinger. However, with less strength removed from my more powerful right hand, it became so dominant that I would yank the club back drastically inside the target line, which caused a premature release of the right hand in the hitting area. This in turn closed the clubface and produced a lot of predominantly left-to-left shots.

I'm not saying that the only correct way to play is with an overlapping grip, because the linkage of the hands really is a matter of personal preference. Some fine players with big hands prefer the interlock grip, just as many with small hands favor the overlap. As they all did in determining what worked best for them, you should give each version an honest try before you make a final decision.

NEUTRAL, WEAK, OR STRONG?

What do these terms mean, and how will they affect your playing?

A neutral grip is one in which the palms are set parallel to each other, the right palm facing the target, the two "V"s formed by the thumbs and forefingers both pointing approximately midway between the chin and the right shoulder. This is how the club is held today by most good players.

In a so-called weak grip, the right palm is angled toward the ground, with the "V"s pointing at or even a little left of the chin. I've experimented with that kind of hold, but found that it restricted the proper rotation of my wrists and hands during the swing. Also, gripping weakly forced my right shoulder to jut out in front of my left as I addressed the ball, so that I was setting up with my upper body open to the target line, which put my swing on an out-to-in path, causing pulled and sliced shots.

Trial and error also has taught me to steer well clear of the so-called strong grip—back of left hand and right palm angled toward the sky, "V"s pointing outside the right shoulder. This type of hold exaggerated the hinging of my wrists, and also forced my right elbow too low, thereby causing my arms and wrists to roll too dramatically clockwise, or on too flat a plane, during the backswing.

Of course, these are only my experiences. Other golfers, especially if they lack strength or "quickness," might well benefit from setting their hands a little more to the right than "neutral." Conversely, the exceptionally powerful player who fights the duck-hook, caused by a very fast rotation of the right hand over the left through impact, could benefit from slightly weakening his grip. Setting the hands a little more on top of the handle removes strength from the right hand, which slows the releasing action, which prevents the clubface from closing quite as fast through impact.

LIGHT OR FIRM GRIP PRESSURE?

Common but confusing advice on grip pressure is to squeeze the grip with the same amount of force necessary to push toothpaste from a tube; or to hold it as gently as if restraining a small and delicate bird; or to grasp it as firmly as if shaking a close friend's hand.

I usually hold the club relatively lightly in both hands, with the maximum amount of pressure in the last three fingers of my left hand. However, I think advising a player to maintain just one grip pressure for all shots is as ludicrous as instructing a guitarist to always strum the chords of his instrument in exactly the same way—either fast or slowly. During a typical round of golf I make long, short, and in-between swings, in order to hit the ball crisply, softly, high or low, depending on such variables as lie, distance, and wind and ground conditions. To do all that requires frequent changes in grip pressure, all the way from very light to very firm, depending on what I'm trying to do with the ball, and particularly on the amount of hand action needed for proper execution. Indeed, I even sometimes hold lightly with one hand and squeeze firmly with the other. However, all of these variations have only one purpose—to preprogram "live" or "dead" hand action into my swing, without consciously having to think about this element as the swing is actually taking place.

As you get deeper into this book, I believe you too will come to appreciate more fully the value of ever-changing grip pressure. But before you begin your own experimenting, let me give you some examples of how this technique works.

For a big drive, my goal is to gently pull the club up to the parallel position at the top of the backswing with my right hand, then whip it through at high speed with a full releasing action of both hands. Gripping lightly with both my left and right hands promotes these techniques by relaxing my forearm muscles and freeing up my wrists, allowing me to make a particularly fluid and powerful release of the clubhead through the ball.

Next, I might squeeze the handle very firmly with all of my fingers to play a low-running chip or a short punch shot, because this adjustment cuts down the hinging action of my wrists and discourages me from "flicking" the clubhead at the ball on the downswing and thereby hitting either a skied or topped shot.

On long putts, I grip the club firmly in my left hand and lightly in my right, the firm left hand stabilizing my left wrist and preventing wavering of the putter blade, while the light right-hand hold allows me to "feel" the swinging of the blade, and to better control the pace of the through-stroke according to the length of the putt.

Varying the pressure in the hands is subtle stuff, and thus an element of technique you should tackle only after building and grooving yourself a basically sound and solid grip. Once you've done that, however, never be afraid to experiment. As I've said before, and will again, it's the only way to become a complete shotmaker.

BALL-TO-TARGET TUNNEL

Chapter 4

GETTING SET

Visiting so many courses around the world, I've encountered a lot of club golfers. One thing is certain about them. They almost always dress well, but their *address* is invariably very sloppy indeed.

An inept or awkward address, or setup, is the chief reason why such a high percentage of players fail to hit the ball either very far or very straight. Please hear me clearly as I say the following: *To a much greater extent than all but the very best golfers realize, the setup predetermines not only the path and plane on which the golfer swings the club, but the quality of his motion at every stage of the action.*

If your goal is to become a consistent shotmaker and scorer, you must build yourself a consistent preswing procedure that enables you to:

1. Thoroughly analyze the requirements of each stroke that confronts you.
2. Select a very specific target.
3. "See" the shot you plan to play to that target in your mind's eye.
4. Step into the shot carefully and confidently.
5. Set the clubface to match your intended flight.
6. Align yourself to complement your clubface aim and desired flight pattern.
7. Adopt a posture that allows you to swing the club in such a way as to execute the shot you have visualized.

If, alternatively, you prefer to treat golf as a lottery and leave such details to luck, then you might as well quit reading right here, because no matter how hard you attempt to master what follows, you will always fail. The reason is that you will be building a house without a foundation, and thus one that will always keep falling apart.

I'll level with you. I once considered aim and alignment, stance and posture insignificant details that were excruciatingly boring both to think about and to try to perfect. Frankly, just hearing the word "setup" put me to sleep. Thus, like so many naive novices, for far too long "I did my own thing" at address, including either slumping over like the Hunchback of Notre Dame or standing as stiff-legged as a guardsman at Buckingham Palace.

To make a long and laborious story short, I finally became so sick and tired of hunting the woods for errant balls that I decided to face one of golf's hardest facts: To swing the club consistently well, you can be your own man only to a very limited extent. In other words, there are certain bedrock basics to the game that have to be mastered if you desire to excel at it. From that day onward, I never said the Spanish equivalent of "phooey" to those fundamentals again. *And that was the single smartest move I ever made as a golfer.*

DEVELOP A CONSISTENT ROUTINE

Some of the more scientifically minded pros I've met on tour claim that, by going through exactly the same preswing routine on every shot, the golfer most effectively prepares his subconscious mind for the best possible repetition of his intended action. According to these players, if the brain recognizes exactly what moves the body intends to make, and the precise order in which each will be executed, the swing flows correctly and automatically without any further conscious direction. Apparently, only when something out of the ordinary occurs, such as extra waggles added to the normal quota, does the subconscious become perplexed. When that happens, the fellows say, the swing short circuits.

Well, I'm certainly no scientist, but I do know that when I stick to one carefully ingrained, highly regimented preswing routine, I *do* make many more good swings than bad swings. And, for that reason, like most others trying to make a living at golf, I have become extremely systematic about this phase of my game. These days, if anything disturbs my preparatory routine, I stop and start all over again right from the beginning. Furthermore, I'm certain that by grooving a correct routine of your own in practice, then putting it to work in play, you too will make far fewer mistakes when you actually start to swing the club.

The next time you watch the top pros on TV—or, better yet, practicing or playing in person—take notice of how very, very carefully and methodically and quietly—they *settle* into their shots. Each player follows a precise, step-by-step preswing routine that ultimately finds him addressing the ball with beautiful balance and the perfect posture for his build and swing style. You can take my word for it that this is a very big factor in why these guys all look so effortlessly machinelike in hitting the ball.

All fine golfers pay great attention to achieving correct posture at the ball because of its influence on both the "geometry" and the mobility of the swing. The angles at the knees and waist are especially important.

Tom Watson
Greg Norman
Jack Nicklaus

Obviously, the players' actual setup routines accommodate various idiosyncrasies. To give examples at both ends of the spectrum, Lanny Wadkins, who has a buzzsawlike swing, takes little time in setting up the ball, while Bernhard Langer, a deliberate person, is very studied in his preparatory routine. I'm somewhere between the two, but the point about all of us is that the procedure, whatever its pace and components, never varies once we have decided it is as effective as we can make it.

BE AS "QUIET" AS YOU CAN

On this subject, I find it interesting that more than a few teachers propose that golfers should play according to their personalities. In other words, if you are quick off the mark in your everyday activities, you should avoid dillydallying over the ball. Conversely, if you're a laid-back type, you should "waltz" rather than "boogie" through your preswing procedure. I'm afraid I don't buy this theory, for one basic reason. To me, the more "quietly" any golfer settles into the setup, the better his chance of getting himself in the correct position to make a precise and powerful swing.

As I see it, the quality of your play, much more than your personality, is what influences the speed at which you go about setting up. Being Spanish and therefore a somewhat temperamental player, my mood constantly changes, sometimes quite dramatically even during a single round. Accordingly, I have to be extremely careful not to let a string either of bogeys or birdies speed up the tempo of my preparatory procedure. It's terribly easy to begin rushing either when you are "on a roll" or when you're trying to make up ground. In fact, at the 1986 Masters, the combination of front-running confidence and adrenaline flow, plus the awareness of Jack Nicklaus's name flashing on the leaderboard as he ran off that fabulous string of final-nine birdies and an eagle, caused me to rush my routine—and fatally so, as it proved.

Coming into the par-five fifteenth hole on the final day, I had the championship in my hands, then threw it away by neglecting to stick to my normal preswing routine. Idiotically, I set up to my second shot and hit the ball before I had clearly decided which was the higher percentage shot—a soft fade with a 4-iron, or a hard 5-iron straight at the flagstick. Indecisive, I made a very poor "quitting" kind of swing with the 4-iron, and the chance of a third Masters vanished as the ball darted left before splashing into the pond fronting the green.

Tragedy struck in an instant chiefly because I played the shot too fast. Nobody beat me but myself. And you know as well as I do that this kind of reality is the hardest to face—whether it's on the golf course or in everyday life.

Still, golf being always such an unpredictable game, we all have to find a way to swallow the sour experiences as well as the sweet ones, and my way has become to try to learn from my mistakes. Thus, flying home to Spain after that Masters, I knew there was only one way to prevent this particular kind of error from happening again.

My preventive medicine is your preventive medicine. Plain and simple, good old practice will prevent you from rushing the setup. The more we ingrain a routine and rhythm of setting up by repeatedly rehearsing our procedures on the driving range and in our casual play, the less we'll be likely to step out of line when it really matters.

THE ULTIMATE SETUP MODEL

For an example of absolute, unvarying meticulousness in setting up to each and every golf shot he plays, I can offer you no better model than Jack Nicklaus. The Golden Bear is living proof that a systematic setup can get you to swing and score better. Jack's ability to stick to a disciplined and deliberate preswing routine through thick and thin, in his driving range work and casual rounds as well as in the heat of the battle, is the major reason he has so many major championships to his credit. No golfer could ever compile such an awesome record, and remain such a factor in his late forties, without absolute self-discipline and systematization in his preparation for every stroke.

I can see Jack now, standing directly behind the ball, staring with intense and unshakable concentration down the fairway. First, he picks the target, the ball's landing area, very specifically, then he selects a mark on the ground a few feet ahead of him directly on that line as his close-up aiming point. Now, he programs himself to make the correct swing by running a mental movie of the ball flying on the line and at the trajectory he has so carefully chosen. Next, he carefully steps into the "golfer's box," always with the right foot easing into place first, and sets the clubhead behind the ball with the face aligned precisely for the type and degree of sidespin he intends to give the shot. Then, carefully looking back and forth from the ball to his interim target, he eases the club and his body into their final positions. Next, he hovers the clubhead slightly above the ground, waggles it lightly a time or two, then sets the center of the face almost flush to the back of the ball and very slightly above the ground. Finally, he's ready to pull the trigger.

Honestly, I could watch Jack practice for hours. The way he works his body into the setup and builds a balanced foundation from the feet upward is really a beautiful sight to a man who aspires to his kind of record. His entire preswing process flows as smoothly and cohesively as a piece by Mozart. If you need a model for your own address procedure, you'd have to look long and hard to find a better one.

Nicklaus credits Jack Grout, his lifelong teacher, with impressing upon him at a very young age the vital importance of a correct setup. And, as good as Nicklaus is today, he is the first to admit how easily a tiny fault can sneak into the preswing process and totally foul up his entire game. That's why he still seeks out Grout at every opportunity—and why they always begin the checkup with aim, alignment, posture, and the other mechanics of the setup. Nicklaus has often said that these account for about 80 percent of good ball striking, and he could be right about that.

I'm honored that Jack says positive things about my setup to the ball. The major similarity between us, aside from our never-ending attempt to adhere to proven fundamentals, is our tempo. If you were to clock us, from the time we select the club to the time we strike the ball, I believe our pacing would be very much the same, give or take maybe a second or two. Nevertheless, I do at least two things differently than Jack.

AIMING AND VISUALIZING

First, as I pointed out previously, Nicklaus prefers to pick a spot a few feet ahead of him on his target line as a key aiming aid, rather than aligning on the distant target itself. He feels strongly that this device adds to his sense of certainty about the correctness of both his clubface aim and his body alignment. Without it, he would feel much less confident over the ball.

I surely can't argue with success, but I've experimented with this method and found it just isn't right for me. When I set up to a "short" target, invariably I start to feel disoriented over the ball, which causes me to lose my imaginative powers. For me, that's like losing my eyesight.

In order to gain the confidence I need to make the swing that will hit the shot I need to play, I must be able to "see"—clearly visualize mentally—a line from the ball all the way to my actual target, both at the start of the setup, as Jack does, and, equally importantly, at the end of my routine. This final "look-see" from ball to distant target is my way of confirming in my mind, one last time, the exact destination of the ball: Something like a ground crew running a final computer check just prior to launching a space rocket. Then, once everything checks out A-okay, my entire body responds by swinging the club almost reflexively in response to the picture of the shot in my mind's eye.

Although I feel a bit like a house painter criticizing Michelangelo, I think the majority of middle-to-high handicap players will do better by lightly soling the club flush to the turf, as I do, rather than hovering it slightly above the ground as Nicklaus almost always does. Jack argues that this rather unorthodox technique prevents him from snagging the club on the takeaway, and also that it helps him start back smoothly and with everything moving in one piece—one of his key lifelong fundamentals. Well, let's face facts, you are not a Jack Nicklaus, which you just might have to be to hold that club steadily above the grass without tensing up at least a little bit. The risk is, in short, that this move will get your muscles so tied in knots that you'll snatch the club away from the ball too quickly, just to relieve some of the tension. Such a startback is a very definite hindrance to becoming a fine golfer.

AVOID UNCOMFORTABLE BALL POSITIONING

Thus far I'm sure I sound pretty orthodox about the technicalities of the setup, and to a certain extent this is true. As I said earlier, there are a number of fundamentals that just about everyone seeking to become a fine player must adhere to. However, when it comes to the position of the ball in relation to the feet, I'm something of a rebel.

Unlike so many American pros schooled to mechanically repeat essentially one set of moves, I rarely play two consecutive shots with the ball identically positioned relative to my feet. Since I'm recognized most for my imaginative shotmaking abilities, this may not come as a surprise. However, I'm not talking about switching ball position to play finesse shots, but simply to play exactly the same "standard" shot I played on the hole before. Why? My philosophy is straightforward: *Never hit a shot with the golf ball in a particular position if it makes you feel even the slightest bit uncomfortable.*

I know this is revolutionary talk, especially since most modern golf instructors like to make so many things about the swing so cut and dried. There are, however, some pretty good reasons for my approach, the biggest one being the importance of comfort over the ball in inducing confidence in the upcoming shot.

Since golf was first played there have been essentially two schools of thought about ball position. The first, of which Jack Nicklaus is perhaps the most successful proponent, proposes that the golfer play every club in the bag pretty much off the inside of his left heel or instep. The other school, of which Arnold Palmer is a star advocate, claims that a golfer will hit a higher percentage of pure shots by playing the driver off his left heel and moving the ball progressively farther back in his stance as he uses progressively shorter clubs. Well, as superbly as those two greats have played the game, I wouldn't give one measly peseta for either of those methods. And, in looking out for your own best golfing interests, I suggest you don't either. Here's why.

When you sit down and really think about it, the simple fact that two golfing immortals use distinctly different systems should tell you that there is no hard and fast rule that dictates the "correct" place to position the golf ball when hitting any one of fourteen golf clubs. Chances are, though—depending on your teacher or the golf magazines or books you've read in the past—you already have adopted one of those methods.

I'd be willing to wager that if you now play every shot off your left heel, you slice or pull-hook a great many wood shots, and here's why. The ball is so far forward that it is very difficult for you to return the clubface to it squarely. Sensing this as you reach the top of the backswing, you lunge your right shoulder forward as the first move of the downswing, throwing the arc of the swing from out-to-in across the target line at impact. If the clubface is open to this oblique swing path as the ball is struck, you hit a slice; if it is square, you hit a straight pull; if it is closed, you hit a pull-hook.

It's likely, too, with the ball opposite the left heel, that you hit many shots "thin" with your short-irons. The reason is that this too-far-forward position prevents you from making contact while the clubhead is still slightly descending—vital to hitting the ball cleanly and crisply and generating maximum backspin.

If you belong to the school that believes in moving the ball back in your stance each time you go to a shorter club, I'd bet that one of your biggest faults is hitting weak and high short- and medium-irons. The reason is that the ball is so far back in your stance that you are forced to swing the club up and down too steeply. This prevents you from properly coiling your upper body in the backswing, which is essential to generate even the minimal amount of power needed to loft these shorter-shafted clubs the correct distance. I'd also bet that you frequently take divots slightly in back of instead of ahead of the ball, which is a sure way to hit it both too high and too short.

I hope you see where I'm heading, which is to suggest that, whenever you lock yourself into one way of positioning the ball for each shot, you are setting yourself up for trouble because you are overlooking one vital fact: As a human being, you are constantly subject to change.

Think about it. Do you wake up every morning feeling strong, supple, confident? If the answer is no, then how can you expect to swing a golf club exactly the same way as you did the day before? I know I don't, and can't.

Some days my body and the club move more slowly than on others, in which case I'll position the ball farther forward to give my sluggish body more time to square up the clubface at impact. Conversely, on mornings when I feel extra supple and my swing speeds up, I compensate by positioning the ball a little farther back, which helps me to stay behind it through the hitting area.

Spending ample time warming up on the practice tee before each round gives me such a good feel for my swing that I can usually sense even the slightest change in its tempo, and am therefore able to make the necessary corrections in ball position before I get out on the course. If you haven't yet reached this stage of golfing self-awareness and self-analysis, you can learn to detect a slower or faster tempo simply by taking note of the ball's flight.

Generally speaking, if your shots fly to the left of the target most of the time, your action is too quick. Conversely, if they drift predominantly to the right, things are happening too slowly.

MY PARAMETERS

Before you see me as some kind of ever-changing chameleon, let me emphasize that I do have boundaries dictating the *general* placement of the ball in my stance. I want to be set up to "sweep" the long clubs, "pick" the medium-irons, and "nip" the short shots off the turf. Remember: *The setup revolves around ball position, and the swing revolves around the setup.*

Depending on the mood I'm in and how I feel physically, I play the longer clubs—driver through 4-iron—anywhere from a point directly opposite my left instep to a point two inches behind my left heel. From this position, I'm able to make a low takeaway, a nice full body turn, and a complete uncoiling of my lower body coming down, with a good extension of the club through the ball after the actual hit.

With the 5- and 6-irons (the two clubs I consider the medium-irons), I position the ball anywhere between my left heel and two inches behind it. The short-irons—the 7-, 8-, and 9-irons, the pitching-wedge and the sand-wedge—I play anywhere from two to seven inches back from my left heel, far enough forward to encourage a smooth takeaway and an adequate turn, but far enough back to encourage a steep enough swing to catch the ball a crisp, slightly descending blow.

The renowned British teacher, John Jacobs, whom I highly respect, suggests you swing every club in the bag without a ball, and that wherever the clubhead begins to brush the grass is the spot you should position the ball. To me that makes a lot of sense, because it allows you to determine approximate ball positions related to your individual build, posture, body suppleness, swing path, and plane of motion. All these factors, however, are subject to change, which is why it's crucial, when you warm up before a round, to try to identify changes in your swing, either by feel or by studying the ball's flight, or a combination of the two. Then go ahead and move the ball around in your stance until you find the best positions for playing the various clubs—i.e., the most effective in terms of solidity and accuracy of strike.

HAZARDS OF AN OVERMECHANIZED APPROACH

Now, confession time.

If you were to ask me after I hit any full shot to tell you precisely how far behind the inside of my left instep I played the ball, I couldn't do it. That's because I depend almost entirely on feel developed through practice, plus instinct, to stay within my ball-position parameters. This is how I have played golf nearly all my life, and it's worked pretty well thus far. I say "nearly" because in 1980 I tried treating the setup and swing as a science, which is when I discovered, for sure, that too mechanical an approach to golf is a very big mistake.

While winning the Masters that year, I was swinging so smoothly that I had high-speed sequence photographs taken of my action. I studied them and made pages and pages of notes for future reference. Indeed, I even went so far as to mark off ball positions, then measure the width of my stance and the distance I stood from the ball. Today, I wish I could forget all about that episode.

Upon returning to Europe, my hot streak continued for a few weeks, then my game suddenly turned cold. This perplexed me because, according to some videotape I had taken of my swing, I was setting up exactly according to the notes made about my magic form at Augusta.

"It just *has* to work," I told myself. But the more I clogged my mind with facts and figures, ultraexact address positions and precise swing angles, the more my game went from bitter to downright sour. Finally, after a rest period at home in Santander, the truth hit me: "Seve, you fool, you're not allowing for changes in tempo, timing, mobility, head movement, hand speed, and, above all, your ever-changing metabolism and mood."

I couldn't believe I had been so stupidly stubborn as to stick rigidly to those notes and photographs, even though doing so caused me both to feel uncomfortable and play increasingly poorly. Against my entire nature, I had made the mistake of trying to become a totally mechanical golfer—a sort of living, breathing, walking, talking version of the famous ball-testing machine "Iron Byron." Thankfully, sense finally prevailed. I tore up all the reference material and returned to my old instinctive way of playing the game.

The lesson is, of course, that no golfer is or can become a robot, so that treating the swing totally as a science or an exercise in physics is almost always counterproductive. In fact, it's my view that striving too hard for "mechanical" perfection has hurt many more golfers than it has helped, including some potentially very fine ones. And I believe this is particularly true of America, where there is a certain mind-set that believes a purely technological answer exists for just about everything.

Sure, you need to build a firm foundation based on certain proven fundamentals. But never become too rigid about following any specific "geometry" in your approach to any aspect of golf. Rather, let common sense and the "feel" that comes from practice and experience guide you from day to day. And do so particularly with the position of the ball in relation to your feet.

Now, let's move on to the other fundamentals that will enable you to put your body and club in the most *workable* position at address from which to make a fine golf swing. To help you to best understand how each element of the setup fits flowingly into this overall preswing preparatory process, I am going to do this by walking you through my own routine.

THE SETUP: STEP-BY-STEP

Step 1: Targeting

Having carefully analyzed the shotmaking challenge facing me, and selected the most suitable club for playing the required stroke, I start my setup procedure from a position directly behind the ball, with my first concern being to clearly identify what I think of as my "final target." When hitting a drive or a lay-up shot, my final target is a small, carefully calculated area of the fairway. Owing to my aggressive nature, the flagstick, rather than the fat of the green, most frequently is my final target on approach shots from the fairway and on par-three tee shots, unless it is so dangerously situated that to go directly for it could be suicidal.

My natural shot flies slightly from right to left, so most of the time in setting up I must build in an allowance for the ball to draw gently back from my aiming point to my final target. Since I intend to teach you how to hit the same strong, distance-generating flight pattern, I'd like to think you will soon be making the same allowances.

Exactly where I want to aim the clubface and start the ball is determined by the hole's shape, its hazards, the wind, the position of the flagstick, and, finally, by an honest self-appraisal of how well my draw is working on any particular day.

Once I pinpoint my final target, I actually "see" in my mind's eye a kind of tunnel stretching from the ball to that area or point, which, when it appears, has the effect of blocking everything else from my mind.

Step 2: Rehearsing

Still standing directly behind the ball looking down my "tunnel," I make one leisurely practice swing to rehearse my swing triggers and to help me relax. During it, in order to get the fullest possible sense of the desired upcoming motion, I usually close my eyes.

Closing my eyes during the practice swing greatly intensifies the feel of my right-hand and right-hip swing-triggering or swing-initiating action. Once the practice motion is properly started, continuing to swing "blind" heightens my sense of the body and club working cohesively as a team in completing the rehearsal.

Try practice swinging with your eyes shut whenever you want to get the maximum sense of the motions of the golf swing.

Step 3: The Right Foot

Stepping now into the shot from the side, I continue to glance at the final target to preserve and reinforce my sense of the "tunnel" running from the ball to my aiming area or point. Next, I plant my right foot, setting it very nearly perpendicular to my imagined ball-to-target line. Where my foot points may seem like a minor detail, but, in fact, it's extremely important to me. The almost-square right-foot position I prefer encourages the upright backswing I desire, in that the foot acts as a strong backstop to prevent my hips from either overturning going back or "spinning out" coming down.

Step 4: Aiming the Clubface

My next move is to set the clubface behind the ball looking absolutely squarely at *my aiming point*, a maneuver that greatly boosts my confidence about making the swing that will send the ball to the chosen target. If I'm not sure I've selected the correct aiming point, I walk away and start again, and so should you. Too many golfers think their shots will just "work out" from a casual or generalized aim. Most of the time they won't.

Step 5: Completing the Stance

Now I jockey my left foot into position, angling it targetward about twenty degrees from perpendicular while keeping my shoulders, hips, and knees square or parallel to the target line.

Let me clarify this a little more. In a square stance, a line across the toes runs parallel to the direct ball-to-target line—the two, if drawn, look just like a set of railroad tracks. In an open stance, a line across the toes angles *left* of the target line, while in a closed stance a line across the toes angles *right* of the target line.

What about the width of my stance—the distance apart of my feet? We are all built differently and feel is subjective, so I won't give you answers in feet and inches, but rather some guidelines.

Spread your feet about as wide apart as the width of your shoulders at the insides of your heels to play a 5-iron, then progressively widen the stance for longer clubs and narrow it for shorter ones. Remember, a fairly wide stance enables you to make a wider backswing arc and thus create a more powerful sweeping action through the ball at impact with the longer clubs. A narrow stance, on the other hand, encourages a more upright swing, which is the easiest way to ensure that you hit slightly down on the ball with the shorter irons.

In going through this routine, I try always to stay lively on my feet, easing them around and moving them up and down until I feel, first, fully comfortable with my ball position; and, second, am certain that my hands hang naturally with my arms extended in a relaxed fashion from my body, with all of the clubhead's sole except the far toe end lying flush to the turf. Once I'm satisfied about those factors, my concerns turn to posture.

Step 6: Posture

Let me set the scene here by telling you that the statement often made in golf books and magazines, that "at address you should be trying to mirror the impact position," is in my view total nonsense. There is just no way to effectively preset the extremely "active" impact position of a powerful golf swing from the distinctly "passive" address position of a correct setup.

The key to good posture is arranging your body in a *balanced and athletic position.*

Flexing my knees slightly and leaning my torso forward from the hips with a relatively straight back allows me to distribute my weight evenly between the ball and heel of each foot. That enables my feet to serve as flexible stabilizers, rather like the foundation studs in a well-designed building.

I arrive at my most efficient angle of incline toward the ball by trying to stand about halfway between the soldier's "attention" and "at ease" positions. I want to be neither too tense nor too relaxed; to feel that I'm standing "tall," but not so tall as to eliminate a keen sense of springiness in my legs.

To finalize my ideal setup position, I'll run a fast check over the other elements vital to good posture—left shoulder higher than the right, rear end out, chin up—with a particular concern that I'm not exaggerating any of them. However, I'm very aware of one crucial setup factor that will never just fall into place, regardless of how naturally I stand, which is the position of the hands in relation to the ball.

When playing woods or medium- or long-irons, I normally set my hands directly in line with—perpendicular to—the ball, to encourage a low sweeping takeaway directly along a rearward extension of the target line. That's because I usually want to hit these clubs with the cleanest possible sweeping action, which requires the clubhead at impact to be traveling on a shallow ellipse. In contrast, when setting up to play short-irons I set my hands slightly in front of the ball to better promote a more U-shaped arc and thus a more descending blow. With all clubs, I make a conscious point of avoiding any upward arching of the wrists, especially the left wrist, as this will most assuredly prevent my hands from working as fluidly and freely as I need them to.

Step 7: Final Grip Check

Once my hands are set in position, I make sure that my grip is still correct by checking on the "V" alignments discussed in the previous chapter. Also, I check that my left arm and the clubshaft form a straight line from my left shoulder to the ball.

Because it is essentially "passive," the address position is necessarily very different from the highly "active" position the fine golfer arrives in at impact. So, in setting up, don't make the mistake of trying to match your hitting position. Instead, set up in a manner that gets your club and body aimed correctly, then promotes swinging naturally "through" rather than "to" the ball.

Step 8: Head Back

With the ball positioned forward in my stance, I rotate the tip of my chin slightly to the left so that it points to a spot an inch or two behind the ball, which has the effect of tilting my head and upper body slightly to the right. This maneuver serves two purposes. First, it assists in smoothly activating my right side, encouraging the clockwise turning of my right hip that is part of the triggering of my backswing. Second, it helps me keep my upper body behind the ball until the last possible moment before impact, an absolute must for generating maximum power with all the clubs.

As a guideline, a vertical line drawn from the back of the ball would practically dissect my left shoulder when playing the ball off my left heel. This same line would run through my left ear when I play short-irons just about in the middle of my stance, which is more or less my normal ball position for making the slightly descending blow necessary with those clubs.

I keep my chin well free of my chest, to provide plenty of room for my left shoulder to swing freely beneath it in the backswing, and for my right shoulder to follow suit in the downswing.

Step 9: The Final Checks

Once I feel mechanically correct in my setup, yet totally comfortable and "ready" muscularly, I make only one final ball-to-target check. That is a very intent look down my imaginary ball-to-target "tunnel," during which I "see" the shot come to life in my mind's eye one last time before I swing.

Finally, I mentally rehearse my right-side swing trigger—the gentle pulling action of my right hand—to give myself the best chance of starting the swing correctly. And I concentrate so hard on that vital initiator that I can actually "see" it operating in my mind's eye as clearly as I can "see" my target at the end of my "tunnel."

Step 10: Finale

I pull the trigger.

After mentally rehearsing my swing triggers, I begin the swing by gently pulling the club away from the ball with my right hand.

Chapter 5

THE ACTION

I now have given you all of what I regard as the vital steps in setting up to the ball correctly. But the setup, although important, is only a foundation. Unfortunately, a perfect setup does not at all guarantee that you will make a perfect golf swing.

To hit good golf shots consistently you must learn how to make a particular swing with the club you have in your hand at the moment. You must make each swing at the tempo and speed that is correct for you, moving the club away at the proper pace, then, after reaching a good position at the top, making a smooth transition into the downswing. You must do this each time with confidence. That means the *trust* that everything you have done to that point ensures that a good forward swing and a fine shot will result *reactively*.

That's what this chapter is all about: Showing you how to swing into and through the correct positions the most natural and effective way possible.

To help you learn to swing this natural way, my plan is to first take you through both the conscious and reflexive stages of my full-length action, the one I employ to hit drives, fairway wood shots, long-irons, and medium-irons, after which I'll cover the subtle differences that occur in my short-iron swing. Before doing so, however, it is important that you have a grasp of the two elements of the swing, long or short, into which all the mechanics of the action must fit perfectly. One is the overall "shape" of the swing, as represented by its plane. The other is the quality of its motion, as represented by its "tempo."

THE CORRECT SWING PLANE

The simplest way to comprehend the plane of the golf swing is to imagine that, at address, your head is poking through a hole in a large, inclined pane of glass that rests on your shoulders at its top and on the ground just beyond the ball at its bottom end. Basically, you should swing the club back and up on this plane or slightly below it—but never *above* it. This mental visualization was one of Ben Hogan's well-known keys for swinging on the proper plane, and to me there remains none better.

The plane's angle is determined by two factors: the geometry of the club you set behind the ball, and the individual physical characteristics that govern your posture at address. In general, the shorter and thus more upright the club, the steeper its angle of inclination as you address the ball and, therefore, the more upright the swing plane. Conversely, the longer and thus flatter the lie of the club, the shallower the angle of its inclination at address and thus the less upright the swing plane.

As we have seen earlier, height and body structure largely determine how you stand to the ball. Usually, the shorter and stockier you are, the farther away from it you will stand and the shallower your swing plane will then naturally be. Conversely, if you are tall and slender, you will tend to stand closer to the ball and to naturally swing the club on a more upright plane.

These are generalities, and you should go with a swing plane that is natural to and compatible with your body type. But try also to stay as close as possible to the guidelines I'm about to give you.

If you flatten your swing dramatically by allowing your arms and the club to fall well below your "natural" plane, you will have to work extremely hard to return the clubface square at impact. Even the best flat swingers I know—and I'm talking about pros with flexible bodies and the time and strength to hit countless practice shots—seem to encounter lots of slumps, hitting shots wildly off-line for lengthy spells. To me, that happens because they invariably swing their arms on much the same rotary backswing plane as the one on which their shoulders are turning, thereby moving the club drastically inside the target line—indeed, such a player's hip turn can become so rounded that he appears to be swinging inside a giant teacup. From such a contorted position, he finds it very hard to fully uncoil his hips in the through-swing and thereby provide a clear path for his arms to deliver the clubface squarely to the ball at impact.

For this reason, I believe *all* golfers should direct their arms *upward* rather than around the body in the backswing, as their shoulders turn or coil on a *slightly flatter* plane. (Compare the arm swing and shoulder turn planes in the sequence photos of my driver swing in the color section.) However, it is crucial that you don't confuse an upright arm swing with a straight-up arm swing, because that will have you simply lifting the club abruptly skyward, which produces a powerless chopping motion on the downswing.

THE PROPER TEMPO

With that concept of swing plane in mind, I want us now to look at perhaps the most critical ingredient in any golf swing, long or short: tempo. The definition of the word in a musical sense is "the relative rapidity or rate of movement." To me, that also stands in a golfing sense in that the parts of the swing must always happen in sequence, at the right time, and in total harmony with one another. *Timing* is another golfing word for this most vital of swing ingredients.

The speed of the swing and its tempo often are confused, largely because the two factors are virtually inseparable. Too much speed, or too little, can ruin the harmony element—the way the parts of the swing work together.

The key is to discover the tempo that is correct for *you*, which basically means finding the maximum speed at which you can swing and still remain in total command of your body and the club. Some very fine players, such as Greg Norman, Bernhard Langer, Lanny Wadkins, and Tom Watson, swing fast; while others—most notably Lee Trevino—by comparison swing much more slowly. Nevertheless, every top professional swings with the tempo—*his* ideal tempo—that allows him *repeatedly to meet the back of the ball with the center of the clubface squarely aligned to the target and traveling at speed.*

The thought of correct tempo should always be in the back of your mind as you work on your swing mechanics because poor tempo frequently nullifies even the best of them. However, the comforting fact here is that developing good tempo becomes a lot easier when you have good mechanics.

Bad mechanics, on the other hand, invariably create bad tempo, simply because they make the swinging action so anatomically awkward and stressful. Most often, the root of the problem lies somewhere in the player's setup. For example, a faulty grip can result in poor positions on the backswing and thus a too fast or too slow tempo on the forward swing. The player who grips the handle too loosely tends to swing the club solely with his hands, and thus quicken his tempo coming down in a vain search for power. The player who grips too tightly is unable to work his hands and arms properly, thus creating a ponderous and/or jerky tempo.

Other setup mistakes can cause similar problems, so, whenever you sense your tempo is out of whack, always check your preswing fundamentals first.

Work on determining your own ideal tempo by experimenting with the speed or pace of your swing components until you find the combination that permits full control, time and again, over your body and the golf club. Keeping your body as free of tension as possible, swing faster and faster until you stop making solid contact and/or your shots start flying wildly. Then throttle back to a speed of swing that enables you, once again, to produce powerful, well-directed shots. Then "feel" and mentally record that perfect personal tempo. Thereafter, keep practicing at "your pace" until eventually it becomes second nature.

THE LONG-CLUBS SWING

The Takeaway

The swing begins at the beginning. That may sound obvious, but it's a fact and a factor that too many higher handicap golfers overlook. I cannot emphasize too strongly the importance of starting your swing in the correct manner.

If the upright arm swing that I recommended earlier is to be effective on the big shots, the arc on which the clubhead swings must be as wide as possible. That can only be accomplished by fully extending the arms and club back together in the initial stage of the swing, or takeaway. The ultimate shape of the swing is determined here, and its overall rhythm is established by the tempo of the movement. That's why I depend on my natural hand—my *right*—to pull the clubhead away from the ball, while at the same time essentially maintaining the triangle formed by my arms and shoulders at the address position.

My right-hand-directed takeaway is uncommon, if not unique, which truly surprises me. It seems so easy to me to use my "natural" hand to gently pull the club away wide and low to the ground starting back from the ball. And that rearward brushing action is the key to promoting "sweep" on full shots—getting the clubhead to "brush through" the ball in the impact zone. Besides that benefit, I think it's far easier to control and pace the speed of the takeaway with my right hand than with my left. And, make no mistake, a slow, smooth start is a most critical factor in the swing, in that it is vital to the steady building of acceleration while permitting maximum control of the club.

Utilizing my right hand as an ignition key of sorts is not the only singular thing about my takeaway. Rather than keeping the back of my left hand facing the target as long as possible, as do many of my fellow professionals, I gently turn mine in a clockwise direction as I pull the club quietly away from the ball with my natural hand. By the time both of my hands have passed my right leg, the back of my left hand and the palm of my right are parallel to the target line, or set precisely in the position all good players strive for when they reach the top of their swings. I believe this "quick-set" component of my takeaway is the main reason I arrive so repetitively in the correct position at the top, and thus am able to repeat the same swing time after time. And, of course, as we have said before and no doubt will again, repeatability is really what good golf is all about.

I certainly would never argue with the success of those top players, including most notably at present Greg Norman, who keep the back of the left hand square, or perpendicular, to the target longer into the takeaway. Nevertheless, because of the great strength demanded by that type of move, plus the hours of grueling practice and stressful mental discipline needed to repeat it effectively, my recommendation is that you avoid copying it.

The typical club player trying to employ this kind of "ultra-square" takeaway frequently makes one of three errors, all of which ultimately cause the ball to slice. Most commonly, he resists the natural tendency for the wrists to hinge, thus becoming so stiff-armed that his hands can't release effectively in the hitting

As I guide the clubhead gently back (low to the ground principally with my right hand), I allow my left hand to rotate in a clockwise direction until, as the clubhead reaches nearly thigh height, its back is facing the target line. I believe this is critical to setting the club in the correct alignment at the top of the swing—and thus, reactively, at impact.

area, with the result that the clubface arrives at the ball both weakly and open-aligned right of target. Alternatively, he turns his left hand so drastically in a counterclockwise direction that the clubface tends to swing from a shut to open position. Third, he severely dips his left shoulder, and in doing so creates the classic reverse pivot, with the weight moving to the left on the backswing and to the right on the forward swing, resulting in a powerless upward hit with an open clubface, plus an ungainly loss of balance.

Regardless of how differently top players initiate their swings, one common factor is the *deliberateness* of the motion. The reason for it is that, the less you force or hurry the action at the start, the better the vital coiling and uncoiling of the body mates with the swinging actions of the arms, wrists, and hands. As my British teacher friend, John Jacobs, told me several years ago, "That, Seve, is what makes for a perfectly timed golf swing and square, solid, powerful clubface-to-ball contact."

At the initial stage of my full swing, as the club is being piloted slowly back largely by my right hand, I'm particularly careful not to allow any swaying of my legs and hips laterally, or violent twisting of any part of my body in a clockwise direction. The reason is that both of those actions spell big trouble. Swaying invariably causes too upright a backswing arc, so that you hit too steeply down on the ball with an open clubface. Twisting usually produces an overly flat backswing arc, creating a tendency to roll the blade closed—looking well left of target—at impact.

My lower-body action ideally is "quiet" during the takeaway, to the point where my left hip dips very slightly as my spine moves just a shade to the right, causing my upper body to tilt ever so slightly left. This tilt, in addition to setting my spine at the proper angle for my torso to coil or turn correctly, promotes the upright arm swing I constantly seek.

Golfers who prematurely turn their shoulders and/or hips in the takeaway, thereby yanking the club violently behind them, do so because they are trying too hard to get to the inside of the target line in the erroneous belief that, by so doing, they will return the clubhead to the ball from the inside. I never even think about getting the club to the inside, for the very good reason that, once my shoulders start turning on a slightly flatter plane than my arms, it can do nothing *but* swing to the inside. At the same time the blade naturally remains at right angles to the arc of the swing, although the appearance is that it fans open relative to the target line.

To convince yourself that your coiling shoulders will automatically swing the clubhead onto the proper inside path, set up square to a wall, resting the toe end of the clubhead flush to the baseboard or molding. Then, after triggering the swing by gently pulling the club straight back for six or so inches, begin turning your shoulders without excessively twisting your lower body or manipulating the club in any fashion with your hands. You will discover that there simply is no other place the clubhead can swing but away from the wall, which, on the golf course, means to the inside of your target line.

This wall drill will convince you that your turning shoulders, rather than your hands, automatically moves the clubhead progressively to the inside of the target line almost from the moment the backswing begins.

While my shoulders and upper body now begin to wind up or coil, my lower body remains what I can best describe as comfortably taut. The reason is that coiling the upper body against a springily resisting lower body best facilitates the full extension of the left arm-clubshaft unit, which in turn creates a wide, power-building swing arc. Furthermore, by extending fully, you build maximum torque into your turn via the latissimus dorsi, the muscles most responsible for generating power in the golf swing according to a study conducted on PGA Tour players at Centinela Hospital in Los Angeles.

To the Top

As I analyze my action, the takeaway ends and the backswing begins as the clubshaft rises to a point where it *parallels* the ground, midway between the level of my knees and thighs. At this stage of the long swing my feeling is that I'm no longer consciously pulling the club back, but that it's now being directed on the proper inside path by the turning of my shoulders, and on the correct upright plane by the swinging of my arms. Hereabouts, too, is where I feel that my right wrist becomes fully cocked, although I'm sure that, in fact, the cocking action—as the dual-angle swing sequence photographs of me in this book show—actually begins quite early in the takeaway.

It's at about this point, too, that I start *rotating my right hip clockwise*, to clear the way for my arms to swing back and up as freely as possible. This smooth coiling rather than violent spinning or twisting of the hip also encourages my right leg to brace sufficiently to hold the weight that is transferred to it from my left side, as my left leg and knee are pulled inward by the coiling and stretching of my upper body. Bracing my right leg, with the knee cocked a little toward the target, serves as a kind of "wall" for me to wind myself against as I continue swinging back, which is vital to both control over the club and the maximization of the torque that ultimately translates into clubhead speed.

As I coil onto my braced right leg, I feel my left heel wanting to be pulled off the ground. I leave it planted, however, because I'm flexible enough to be able to make a big, powerful windup without needing the added freedom of a rising left heel. Most golfers, and particularly seniors who aren't as loose as they once were, might do better to allow the left heel to rise.

A criticism of my swing has been that I sway my upper body away from the target as the backswing progresses. That is not correct. What actually happens is that my head moves more than most other tournament pros move theirs. However, like everything in my swing, this is a deliberate action made for good reason.

Once my hands have climbed to about chest-high, my head begins to move to the right, away from the target, quite dramatically, in order to allow me to coil my upper body as fully as I possibly can behind the ball. An important point to note, however, is that my braced right leg retains its earlier position, thus preventing any degree of bodily sway. What I'm doing—and what the critics are seeing—is simply a few inches of lateral head

Once the clubshaft parallels the imaginary target line, the club begins to swing upward, in my case directed by my increasingly active right hip–right arm actions.

A braced right leg serves as a kind of "anchor" against which I can powerfully coil my body in the backswing.

movement to facilitate a very full windup of the torso. This freedom of movement in my head and upper body, besides allowing me to make the strongest possible upper-body coiling, also permits my hands and arms to swing easily to create the widest possible clubhead arc. Furthermore, by allowing my head to "give" a little, I reduce the stress on my upper torso, which makes me less susceptible to "golfer's back," an ailment common to players who strain to keep the head absolutely centered during the backswing.

Another aspect of my long swinging action that contravenes some theories is the slight *bending*—not breaking—of my left arm late in the backswing. If amateurs who have been taught that keeping the left arm ramrod straight is a commandment of golf never to be broken are shocked by what happens to mine, they should consider Calvin Peete, the most accurate player on the U.S. Tour in recent years, who has a permanently and severely bent left arm because of a childhood accident. How important can a straight left arm be in the light of his great achievements?

My slight left arm "give" is not a conscious action but the result of pressure exerted on that arm by the momentum or swinging weight of the clubhead. It means that I'm allowing my arms the freedom to swing with relatively little tension, instead of in a wooden or robotlike fashion, and I strongly encourage you to do the same. The freer and less tense your arm swing, the better your chance of returning the club powerfully and accurately to the back of the ball. So never fight a slight bending if that's what it takes to produce smoothly flowing motion.

At the Top

My goals at the top of the swing are to have my hands well behind and above my head, the clubshaft parallel to the target line, my shoulders coiled through about 120 degrees, my hips wound through about 60 degrees, and approximately 60 percent of my weight on my right side. At this point in the swing, my overriding feeling is that I've "turned my back to the target," and also well behind the ball. Another sensation I strive for is that the bottom half of my body is the wooden part of a slingshot while the top half is the rubber band—all stretched back to its limit and ready to snap forward with a smooth but powerful release of energy.

Although my upper-body turn is very full and coiled and taut and torque packed compared to many tournament pros, I believe I shift a lot less weight to my right side on the backswing that most of them do. That's because one of my chief goals is to set myself up for a largely reflexive downswing, by which I mean an automatic or involuntary or unconsciously directed motion to and through the ball. Leaving some 40 percent of the weight on my left foot helps trigger my lower body to start tugging targetward as my upswinging arms reach their apex, which makes for a powerful but smooth transition of motion.

To me, the backswing is all about *slowly and fully gathering oneself*, and the downswing is all about *rapidly uncoiling and releasing oneself*. For that reason I think those teachers who advise

Permitting my left arm to bend naturally, if only slightly, late in the backswing alleviates tension and allows me to have the feeling of really "completing" the backswing.

whispering "one" as the club is swung back and "two" as it is started down are doing their pupils a disservice. Splitting the swing into two parts prompts the golfer to consciously try to pause at the top, which in turn forces him to employ some kind of overforceful movement to launch himself into the downswing. Frequently, the continuity or flow of the swing's essential chain-reaction quality is thereby disturbed, with the end product being faulty clubface alignment and/or lack of clubhead speed at impact.

If I actually tried to pause at the top—literally stopped all momentum—I'm sure the sense I'd have was that my swing was running behind schedule. In response, I'd "cast" the club by prematurely uncocking my right hand, or throw my right shoulder outward, or both. Both of those faulty movements inhibit the free, fluid, flailing action of the arms to the point of destroying their ability to naturally return the clubface squarely to the ball at high speed. Obviously, then, I believe *consciously* pausing at the pinnacle of the swing is never a good idea.

The Forward Swing

Having said all that, to be absolutely honest I do quite often get the feeling of a very slight pause or "wait" at the top of the backswing. However, I also know that, just before my shoulders complete their turn, the lower half of my body has begun pulling me in the opposite direction. As soon as I sense this *tugging*, my right side instinctively "fires" without any conscious direction, recoiling my right hip back in a counterclockwise direction, kicking my right knee inward, and drawing the instep of my right foot strongly downward and inward—the beginning of the chain reaction of virtually involuntary motions that make up the down-and-through swing.

The reason this chain reaction is involuntary—*has* to be involuntary—is that it takes me only about one fifth of a second to get from the top of the swing to impact, which is insufficient time for the neuromuscular system to allow any human being to do anything consciously. Hence, once the downswing is sparked, I'm committed for better or worse to a purely reactive series of movements. If I coil fully and swing the club on the proper backswing path and plane, I'll hit a good shot. By the same token, even if I sense that I'm out of position at the top, there's very little I can do about it on the way down. Which, of course, is why the setup and the backswing are so critically important to all golfers.

The truth is, *after my right side fires like a released catapult, I feel nothing*. From that point on the entire motion runs essentially on automatic, which, of course, is why it feels so wonderfully effortless when it is working at maximum efficiency. Indeed, if I do consciously sense a particular component of the overall movement between the time my right side fires and the moment of impact, I know for certain that I've committed a serious swing fault. (I felt just such a fault—a jutting outward of my right shoulder—on my second shot to the par five, fifteenth hole during the final round of the 1986 Masters. You'll remember, from the earlier description of that shot, how I yanked the ball into water fronting the green and eventually lost the championship.)

Now, despite what I've said, just as looking at a photograph of a jigsaw puzzle helps you put it together, understanding the ideal "form" of the downswing can help you to achieve it, even though you can never direct the effort consciously while it's actually happening. So let me briefly describe the facts—what the camera tells me goes on. That way we can mentally draw a schematic of my downswing which hopefully will make it easier for you to employ one continuous motion that naturally moves you *through* each key position. Here is what actually occurs in my downswing, beginning the instant my right side fires.

1. My left knee starts shuttling *targetward.*

2. My hands and arms *fall* freely, all the way to waist level, into what I call the "hitting slot." At the same time, the club drops into a plane slightly lower or flatter than it was at the top.

3. My left hip starts *clearing*—turning smartly in a counter-clockwise direction.

4. As my weight shifts to the *inside* of my left foot, my right heel rises a hair off the ground.

5. My left shoulder moves *up*, while my right shoulder moves *down.*

6. My left hip clears farther *left*, opening up a clear passageway for my hands and arms to swing the club fast and freely back to the ball from inside the target line.

7. My driving hips and legs increase their thrust, prompting my right heel to rise farther off the ground as weight starts shifting to the *outside* of my left foot.

Here's how my right hip and knee "fire" in response to my lower body tugging me targetward at the start of the downswing.

8. As my hands are pulled downward to thigh level, my right arm-hand unit lags behind my left arm-hand unit, readying itself to transfer its stored power to the clubhead at the last possible moment.

9. My left arm swings freely away from my body, while my right arm makes a sidearm motion, similar to the one I use in skimming a stone across water, traveling on the slightly shallower plane that the club fell into early on in the downswing.

10. As my arms-hands speed increases, centrifugal force on the clubhead becomes so great that it obliges my wrists to start quickly uncocking.

11. As my left hand continues rotating and squaring itself to the target, the clubface does the same.

12. My left leg absorbs almost all of my body weight and, in bracing, provides me with a "wall" to hit powerfully against.

13. As my right side lets loose, all but the ball of my right foot lifts off the turf.

14. My head stays well *behind* the ball as my upper torso resists the targetward pull of my lower body. (This is the natural cause of the so-called "late hit," which really isn't late at all but exactly on time, and thus is key to returning the clubface squarely and solidly to the ball.)

15. At the exact moment of impact, my shoulders have returned to a square position—parallel to the target line—while my left arm and the clubshaft are aligned, and the back of my left hand and the palm of my right are dead square to the target.

This side-angle view of the right side downswing "firing" action shows how my right knee drives inward as I push inward and downward off my right instep, driving the club powerfully toward the ball. I feel the motion is comparable to that of a catapult thrusting a rock through the air.

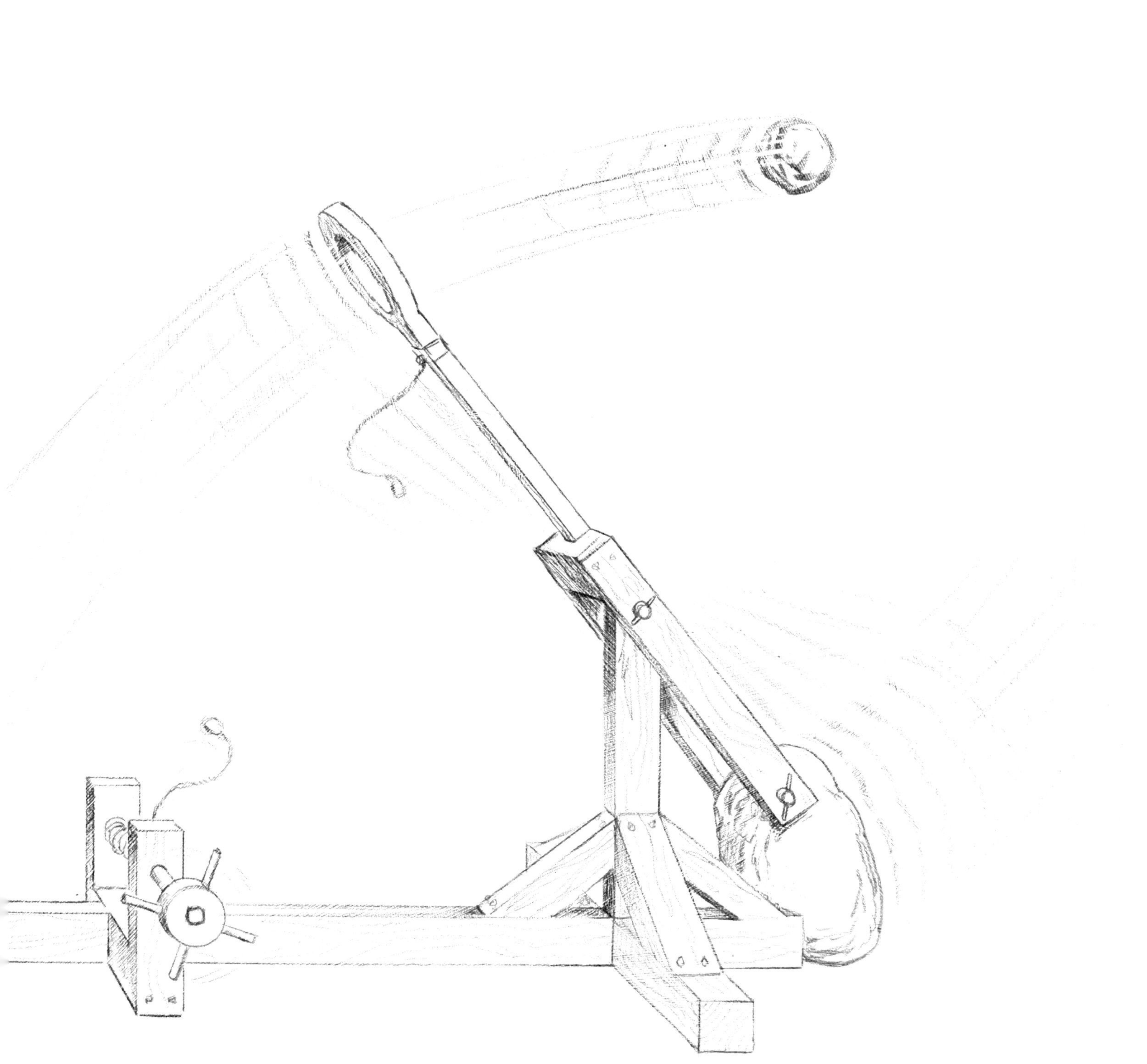

The most critical link in this reactive or reflexive chain is the relationship of my arms and shoulders, and it deserves further comment here. The firing and thrusting actions of my right hip and knee force my head to move slightly downward and farther away from the target. That subtle move in turn encourages my upper body, and most notably my shoulders, to resist the pull of the lower half until my arms have fallen freely down. Hence, my arms are controlling my shoulders, rather than vice versa.

At that point, my right arm starts to move past and away from my body and begins to straighten because of the centrifugal force acting on it. As club nears ball, stored power is transmitted through that arm to my right hand and, finally, to the clubhead, allowing it to whip into the ball at about 120 miles an hour. As I approach the moment of truth, I trust that the ball will be struck cleanly and squarely, for the simple reason that it will be in the path of a good swing.

Now, just reading the above should convince you that the downswing is far too complex an action, and flowing much too fast, ever to be consciously directed. For that reason, it seems to me to be a waste of time for golfers to try to segregate the body-club positions involved and practice them separately. What you probably would find worthwhile, however, is either to work in practice on my right-sided trigger for sparking the downswing, or to seek out and groove a good right-sided start-down trigger of your own. Either way, your goal is to find a move, or a feel, or a thought, which *automatically* promotes swinging through all the key positions that form part of the connected downswing chain.

I've spent more hours meditating on the downswing than any other phase of the swing, and have physically experimented with it commensurately. If there was a way to consciously arrive in all the correct positions and to perfectly direct the clubface to the ball, I believe I would have discovered it by now. Instead, I have convinced myself that there is no way to control the physical movements of the swing by consciously, so to speak, "connecting the dots."

Consequently, I find it very frustrating to see amateur golfers trying to *make* the downswing happen. Unfortunately, many of them commit this fault mostly because they insist on trying to direct the downswing consciously, and often in the process using a less-than-natural, left-side-dominated trigger. For instance, the "lunger," in trying to force his weight over to his left side, drives his left leg overviolently toward the target. The "spinner," in attempting to deliberately clear his left hip, twists it in that direction at the start of the downswing so overaggressively that his entire body spins, often with a total loss of balance. The "puller,"

The more powerfully my right side "fires," the faster and thus more powerfully the club arrives at the ball.

the most common of this breed, yanks down hard on the club's handle, using predominantly his left hand, which to me is like throwing a wrench into the spokes of a spinning bicycle wheel.

I'm not poking fun at high-handicappers here. I simply want to emphasize that these and all the other "false left-sided starts" serve only to disrupt the natural flow and tempo of your downswing, and so will forever prevent you from consistently returning the clubface to the ball squarely at speed.

By now, it is probably plain that my sole mental key to making a well timed, well-coordinated downswing is *trust—believing that correct club-to-ball application is the reflexive culmination of everything I do correctly before the club begins its downward journey.* I suppose, in a way, my downswing operates much like a player piano. Once the instrument is turned on, it plays a melodic tune automatically. Similarly, once my lower body tugs me targetward and my right side begins to fire, I swing melodically *through* all the paramount positions without consciously tinkling the keys.

I'm highly confident—I am full of trust—that the sweetspot of the clubface will find the center of the back of the ball as *my swing automatically carries the clubhead through it.* Indeed, from the time I make the transition into the downswing until I'm well into the follow-through, I'm almost in a state of trance. Photographs may indicate that my eyes focus on the ball, but I never consciously stare at it, so I never consciously witness impact. In fact, on days when my feel for the setup is 100 percent, my internal "eye" for visualizing shots is crystal clear, and my coordination is like clockwork, my eyes actually close as I make contact with the ball, only picking it up flying through the air on the follow-through.

That statement is probably something of a shock to those of you who have been convinced that staring fixedly at the ball is a golfing imperative. If that's the case, I would ask how people like Pat Browne, the blind former world golfing champion, can smoke long drives and break eighty on full-sized golf courses. The answer, of course, is a good setup, a sound backswing, then *total trust* in what follows reflexively.

Only golfers who try consciously to direct the downswing, and consequently hit "at" rather than *swing through* the ball, need to stare at it. Don't you be one of those. It might take some effort to develop a swing that works properly, but the payoff will be extremely worthwhile—not least in the great feeling of trust you will have in the business part of the action thereafter.

The Follow-Through

Just as the nature of the forward swing is determined by the setup and backswing, the finish of the action is ideally a direct reflection of what has gone before, and ideally attained entirely reflexively. Nevertheless, knowing the characteristics of a good follow-through and finish, and conditioning yourself to visualize achieving them, can help promote the kind of free-flowing downswing motion essential to accelerating the clubhead through the ball at maximum controlled speed.

In hitting any wood, long-iron or medium-iron, these are the key positions I hope to match as I swing through my own follow-through (starting when my hands reach waist height):

1. My left shoulder points skyward as my right shoulder, which has brushed under my chin, points to the ground.

2. My left arm begins to bend at the elbow as my right arm extends fully.

3. The palms and backs of my hands parallel the target line.

4. My left hip clears so fully to the left that the left pocket of my pants becomes invisible from a face-on angle, while my right hip has fired so hard that the right pants pocket, behind my chin at address, is now several inches ahead of my chin.

5. My head, only slightly behind the ball when I assumed the address position, is about a foot behind the point where the ball was before it was struck.

6. My right leg bows inward and flexes, as my left leg braces.

7. Almost all of my lower-body weight shifts to my left foot, with only about 15 percent remaining on my right foot.

Ideally, at the finish of a tension-free swing, my belt buckle faces slightly left of target. Also, I am in a comfortably erect attitude, with 95 percent of my weight balanced on the outside of my left heel and the remainder resting on the toe end of my right foot. Both of my arms are easily folded at the elbows, as my hands come to rest at a point level with my head and behind my left ear. All these positions are indications that I have swung freely and forcefully, yet well enough within myself to be in complete control of my body and the club.

SOME EVERGREEN TIPS ON FULL-SWING TECHNIQUE AND TEMPO

TRIGGERING THE SWING

Most professional golfers and teachers believe that the swing should never begin from an absolute dead stop, and therefore favor a *forward* press of some sort to trigger or initiate the action. For instance, Tom Watson sets up with his hands level with the ball, then presses them forward slightly and starts the backswing from there. Gary Player cocks his right knee targetward a little, then goes on the rebound, so to speak.

I've tried a variety of such triggers, but all they seem to do is quicken my natural swing tempo. However, that doesn't mean they won't work for you. If you find yourself freezing over the ball, try experimenting with different forward presses until you discover one that smooths things out.

KEYS TO A GOOD TAKEAWAY

If you've developed the bad habit of yanking the club drastically inside the target line, or lifting it up abruptly at the start of your takeaway, or both, visualize a tee peg planted in the ground about eighteen inches directly behind the ball on an imagined rearward extension of your target line. Then try to brush the tee away with the clubhead as you swing back.

Another practice aid to promoting a sweeping takeaway, and thereby a sweeping hit, is to sole the clubhead several inches behind the ball and start the swing from that point.

INSURING COILING

Very few amateurs coil their upper bodies fully behind the ball at the top of the swing, with the result that they have nothing to "unwind" coming down, with the result that their shots lack zip, distance, and accuracy.

To help you get the feeling of truly "winding the spring" going back, practice with a golf ball wedged firmly under the outer instep of your right shoe. Set up like that, it is virtually impossible not to get the feeling of coiling your upper body against the resistance of your lower body.

Ingrain that sensation, and its accompanying moves, and golf could become a whole new game for you.

CONTROLLING THE CLUBHEAD PATH

The clubshaft's position at the top of the backswing generally indicates the direction in which the ball will start.

If the shaft points left of the target in what is known as the "laid-off" position, you will most likely deliver the clubhead from out-to-in across the target line and start the ball left (any curving it does will be the result of the interaction of the clubface alignment with the out-to-in swing path).

If the shaft points right of the target at the top, in an "across-the line" position, the forward swing arc will likely return the clubhead to the ball from inside to outside the target line, which will most likely start the shot right.

For a straight shot, then, the clubshaft at the top should parallel the target line.

REGAINING LOST TEMPO

No matter how "grooved" a player's tempo, occasionally he will lose it. The symptoms of an overly slow or deliberate tempo are shots that fly weakly to the right. Shots that start left and keep going that way, or start left then slice badly, are usually signs of too fast a tempo. Let's look at some antidotes to each.

Excessive tension at address, especially in the arms and legs, promotes a robotlike, stilted type of backswing with too slow a tempo to provide adequate clubhead speed at impact. A couple of years ago I experienced that very problem, but fortunately solved it quickly with the help of teaching pro David Leadbetter. Here's his unique tip for players who suffer from an overly slow tempo because of excessive tension.

Imagine you are standing on very thin ice, and try to set up to the ball in an appropriately relaxed manner, feeling exceptionally light on your feet. You want to stand in such a way that you do not crack the ice, or with a pronounced feeling of "lively" balance. In a sense, this will "oil" your muscles just enough to speed up your swing a little, which enhances the correct sequence of motion, enabling you to swing more smoothly and with good acceleration through the impact area.

A good practice drill for breaking down tension is to tee up a dozen balls a few inches apart in a row, step up to each ball quickly but smoothly assuming your address, then swing and hit each one, working nonstop until all the balls are gone. The late Sir Henry Cotton, the renowned British champion, was very fond of this drill, both for teaching tempo and strengthening and training the hands.

Golfers obsessed with power often yank the club up way too quickly on the backswing, then hit down hard *at* the ball—rather than *through* it—on the forward swing. If that's you, try incorporating a one-piece waggle into your preswing routine. Move the club back low to the ground for about a foot, with the arms, hands, and clubhead traveling as a unit before you set it back down behind the ball for the real thing. You'll find that this promotes a slower takeaway, a much smoother tempo, a shallower backswing, and a wide sweeping action through the impact zone.

To develop less "hit" and more "swing," do some practicing with plastic wiffle balls. Because they fly so short, they get your psyche off the power kick and more onto making solid contact. An hour's work a week with wiffle balls is a sure way to smooth out your tempo, which will get you hitting the ball so squarely you won't ever want to swing out of your socks again on the golf course. And just watch those scores drop then!

ACHIEVING SQUARE IMPACT

Straight golf shots are produced by the clubhead momentarily traveling along the target line at impact, on its way from inside that line to inside again, with the clubface looking squarely at the target.

Long golf shots are produced when the above happens and the clubhead is traveling very fast. However, even if you swing the clubhead at 150 miles per hour, if its face isn't square at impact the ball will fly relatively short, as well as badly off-line. To prove this to yourself, set a club down to a ball with its face wide open and swing hard, then set the club squarely to the ball and swing smoothly *within* yourself. The relative distances and trajectories will tell you all you need to know about the "ballistics" of the game.

To promote square, solid clubface delivery, work on setting your right hand, wrist, and arm in the *waiter's tray position* at the top of the swing. In looking at the down-the-target-line view of me in this position (right wrist cocked; right elbow tucked relatively close to my body and pointing at the ground), you should—if you imagine my right hand open and off the club—almost be able to visualize me holding a tray.

The proper downswing action of the right arm is very similar to that used in throwing the ball underhand, and it is much easier to repeat this action in the downswing if you have allowed your right arm to fold into the classic waiter's tray position.

I believe it is easier to make a smooth transition from backswing into downswing, and deliver the club squarely into the back of the ball at high speed, when you arrive at this classic "waiter's tray" position at the top of the swing.

THE POWER-FADE

My right-sided swing produces a slight right-to-left draw as my bread-and butter shot, which adds about 25 yards of roll to the 250 yards of carry I usually get on drives. However, in early October 1987, just prior to the Ryder Cup Match, I faced up to a big problem with my driving game.

On long holes with narrow fairways bordered by deep rough and dense trees, my driving statistics showed that I missed the short grass about 50 percent of the time. That was obviously costly to both my pocketbook and my pride in its effect on my day-to-day tournament play. Even worse was what it augured for my chances in the U.S. Open, which is always played on very tight courses with severe rough guarding the narrow fairways.

Why was I missing so many fairways? The answer is that my right hand is so strong that when I try extra hard to power the ball, I'm inclined to roll it over my left hand too quickly in the impact zone. That causes the clubface to turn over, or close, turning my usually soft, controlled draw into a violent duck-hook.

So why didn't I just rein in and quit letting out the shaft on long, narrow holes? The first answer is that just worrying about the problem plagues my subconscious and makes me tend to overcompensate, swinging too slowly and failing to move aggressively enough through the ball and fully release my hands, which blocks shots to the right. The second answer, plain and simple, is that my game is a mixture of emotion and technique: I *like* to go for the big drive on long holes, tight or otherwise.

How did I cure my problem? Well, I still enjoy experimenting with various swings; if I don't physically try out a particular technique on the practice tee, I will toy with it mentally from time to time, weighing its feasibility. And it's a good thing I've still got a little of the inventor left in me, otherwise I'd never have had the incentive or the ability to perfect a new technique that produces a "power-fade"—an aggressively hit but controlled left-to-right shot.

This new shot enables me to go after the ball with a lot of confidence because, even if I'm a little off in execution, the ball still finishes far down the fairway a high percentage of the time. Thus, on especially tight courses, or on particularly long and narrow holes, the power-fade is the perfect call in that I can let the swing rip fearlessly.

To hit the shot, I begin by teeing the ball slightly higher than normal—the entire ball is a shade above the top of the clubface—and positioned directly opposite my left instep. Next, I align my feet, knees, hips, shoulders—and the clubface—to the left, essentially on the line on which I want the shot to start. Then I weaken my hold on the club just a little by turning both hands slightly to the left, before squeezing the handle a bit more firmly with my entire left hand, which encourages both a delayed release and a less early rotation of the hands.

Once nicely settled into my new setup, I use essentially my normal swinging action, the only real differences being that I hold on a little longer with my left hand in the hitting area (which again delays the rotation of my right hand over my left), and I catch the ball more on the upswing. Mind you, I still release through the shot, but it's a split-second later than usual. This delay, plus the insurance of the firm, weak grip, enables me to make a free and confident swing without fear of the ball going dead left.

The result is a ball that shoots hard off the clubface, gets up quickly, and levels off into a penetrating trajectory as it fades gently back to its final target.

Staying well behind the ball through impact, while bracing my left side, allows me to hit powerfully up on the ball with the driver—a lot like Sugar Ray Leonard solidly planting his left foot on the canvas in order to deliver a big uppercut.

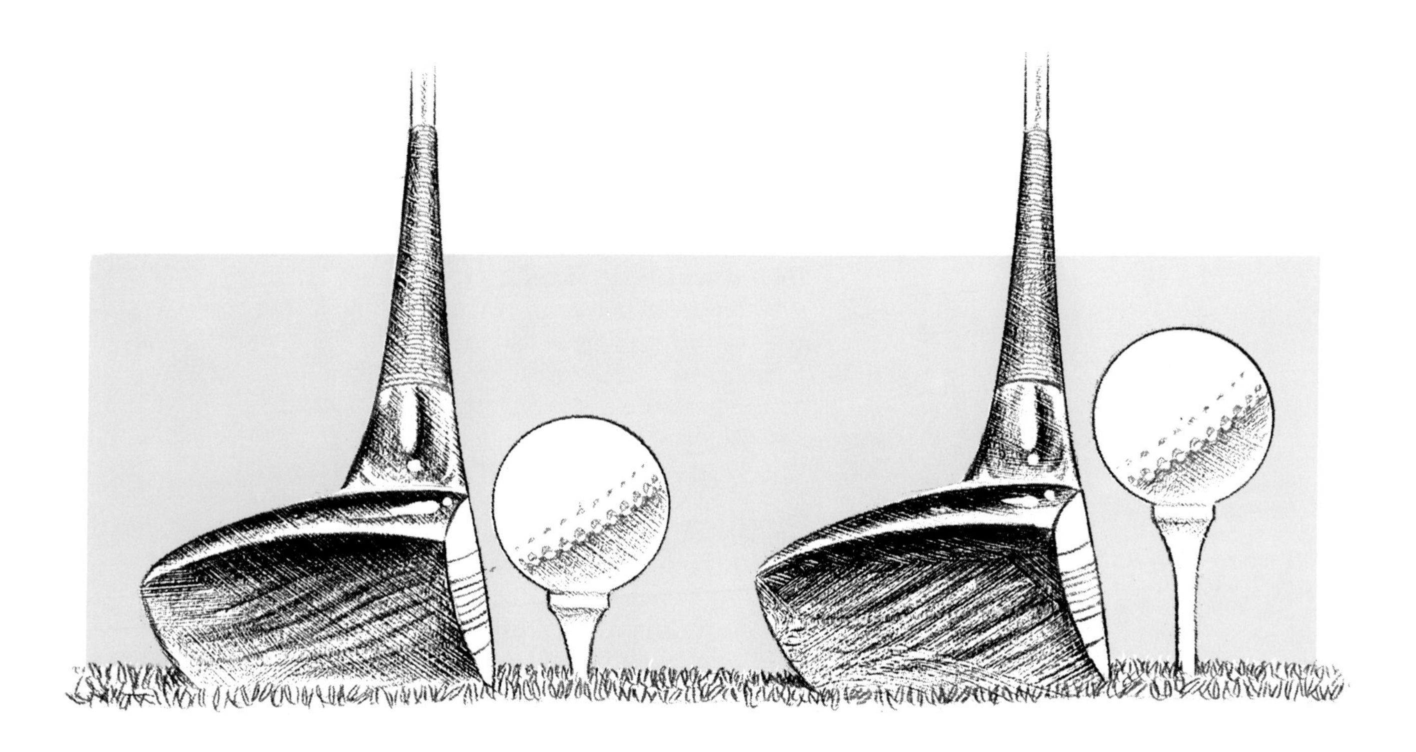

To hit a power-fade with the driver, I tee the ball a little higher than normal to promote catching it slightly on the upswing.

THE SHORT-CLUBS SWING

The 7-iron through the sand-wedge are short in the shaft and heavily lofted in the clubface, which makes them easier to swing and control than the longer clubs. Many amateurs, however, fail to capitalize on these characteristics by rushing their shotmaking visualization process, setting up sloppily, or swinging on too flat a plane.

The typical high-handicapper facing a short-iron to the green often gets lackadaisical simply because the shot looks so easy. The truth is that the closer to the green you are, the more thoughtful and precise the evaluation required, if only because you are trying to get the ball close to the hole. Consequently, you should concentrate even harder on your analysis and planning, not only to be sure you pick the correct shot and the proper club to execute it with, but to reinforce your confidence in being able to do so.

I hit the short-irons, or what I call the "control" clubs, from relatively close range, normally between 160 yards for the 7-iron to 90 yards maximum for the sand-wedge. To produce the greatest possible accuracy with them, I do some things differently in both my setup and swing, relative to the longer clubs.

The Setup

I position the ball far enough back in my stance to naturally set my hands slightly ahead of the face when I sole the club squarely to the target. This hands-ahead position promotes a steeper takeaway, which quickly establishes the more upright swing plane needed to return the club crisply downward into the back of the ball. Normally, the more lofted the club the farther back I position the ball, with the limit being the middle of my stance, unless I'm seeking to impart extra-heavy backspin, about which more later.

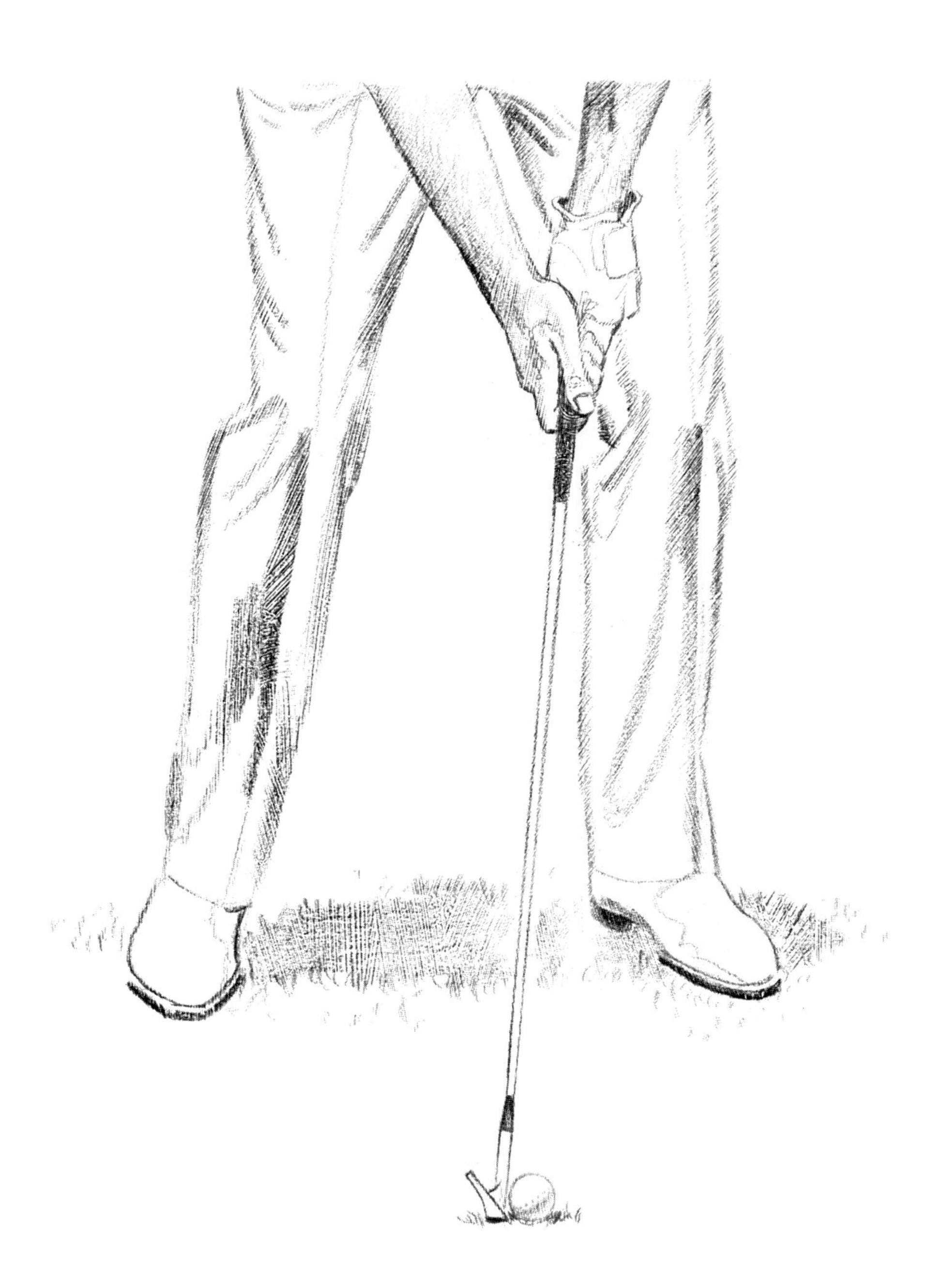

Setting my hands slightly ahead of the ball at address helps me swing the short-irons on a slightly more upright plane than the longer clubs, as well as promoting solid ball-turf contact.

With the longer clubs I have a sense of comfortably reaching for the ball. With the shorter ones the space between my body and the ball is considerably reduced as, responding naturally to the more upright lie of the club, I simply move closer to the ball, which gives me an ever-stronger feeling of being fully in control of myself and the club.

To promote a short, firm kind of swing, along with the upright plane I want, I switch from a square to a slightly open setup, aligning my feet, knees, and hips a little left of the target. Instead of balancing my weight evenly between both feet, I set a preponderance of it left, and, finally, I take a slightly narrower stance than usual—both of these adjustments again being to create maximum control.

KEEP YOUR CHIN UP

A steady head is critical to hitting short-irons accurately, but the typical high-handicapper often overdoes the "head-down" advice, principally by dropping his chin too low at address. This prevents the left shoulder from freely rotating under the chin on the backswing, and the right shoulder from doing the same on the downswing, which distorts the swing path, which produces off-target hits.

To promote a free-flowing arm swing and a down-and-through action in the impact zone, position the tip of your chin a few inches from your sternum or breastbone as you assume your setup, then keep it there throughout the swing.

The Backswing

The setup I've described promotes a narrow backswing arc on an upright plane. For me, however, achieving that "shape" is so critical to striking the ball while the clubhead is still moving slightly downward that I do a number of other things to promote steepness and uprightness.

According to a sophisticated computerized swing-analyzing machine, I set 65 percent of my weight on my left side at address for the short-iron shots. Then on the backswing I shift only about 10 percent of that weight to my right side, or just enough to promote a fluid hip turn, a free-flowing arm swing, and sufficient leg action via rotation of the knees to enhance rhythm. I feel that the 55 percent of my weight remaining on my left foot encourages my shoulders to work more in a tilting than a rotating pattern during the backswing, which further ensures steepness and uprightness.

This rocking action of my shoulder—left down, right up—naturally propels the club upward. But, to be absolutely sure that I maintain a narrow swing arc, I simultaneously also consciously cock my right wrist as I gently pull the club up with my right hand.

In addition to helping me propel the club upward, rocking rather than rotating the shoulders restricts my body turn, narrows my arc, and shortens my backswing, all of which are good. On short shots, I don't need to create big power through a big body coil and a wide swing arc, and neither do you. The priority is precision—hitting the ball to a very small target around the hole.

The fact that on these short-shot swings my left knee never rotates behind the ball, and the club never swings beyond the three-quarter position, is evidence that I'm compacted—albeit *comfortably* compacted—for maximum control. To me, a three-quarter swing maximizes one's chances of finessing the ball close to the flagstick, even though it might involve hitting more club.

I "rock" rather than rotate my shoulders in making my short swing, because this helps me to propel the club up more steeply into a controlled three-quarter position at the top.

The Forward Swing

On long shots, as I've explained, I feel my lower body tugging me targetward even before I reach the top of the backswing, which sparks the instinctive "firing" of my right side, which triggers the reflexive completion of the rest of the down-and-through swing. Because my short-shots backswing is slower and shorter, and I wind my body less far and less powerfully, the downswing cannot be quite as much of a reflexive action.

To initiate correctly, I consciously push my right hip downward and inward, while guiding the club easily downward with my right hand (any hard pulling will always disrupt my naturally slow swing tempo on these shots, so it is to be avoided at all cost). When I perform these downswing triggers correctly, the following chain reaction occurs:

1. Pressure instantly builds all along the inside of my right foot.
2. My knees begin sliding gently toward my target.
3. My arms, hands, and the club fall essentially straight down.
4. My right shoulder tilts downward, setting me in position to keep my upper body well behind the ball through the hitting area.

That knee slide toward the target is definitely the most crucial step in this sequence, in that it shifts almost all of my weight over to my left foot, which causes my left hip to start clearing targetward, which in turn makes room for my arms and hands to swing the club freely downward and past myself.

Another benefit of this knee slide is that it protects me from coming into the ball at an excessively steep angle, as surely would happen if I were to have no knee motion and the club was simply swung straight down with the arms. The knee slide makes the path of swing sufficiently shallow to avoid hitting "fat" into the ground behind the ball, while also allowing it to be steep enough to nip the ball crisply with a sharp downward blow.

My lower body, then, plays the active role coming down, while my upper body remains passive, and especially my head, which stays well behind the ball. If my head moved even the slightest bit ahead of the ball before impact, my shoulders would spin to the left along with it, instead of returning to parallel with the target line, in which case I'd "come over" the ball and miss the shot to the left.

As the big muscles of my lower body move targetward, I have a pronounced feeling of my arms, hands, and finally the clubhead being *pulled downward*, with my wrists maintaining their cock or set until my hands have dropped just below waist level and my left hip is beginning to clear. Thus, I control the speed of the clubhead, and ultimately the distance of the shot, principally with my lower body rather than my hands. Essentially, the more vigorously I push my right hip downward and inward at the start of the downswing, the faster my arms-hands-clubhead unit moves and the farther I hit the ball.

Unless the ball is buried badly—as, for example, in U.S. Open-type rough or British Open-type heather—and I have to go down after it very forcibly, I try never to consciously pull hard with

My targetward knee slide is the most critical move in the downswing sequence, in that it promotes hitting *through* rather than *at* the ball.

my hands. Moreover, even when I do decide to hit a "handsy" trouble shot full out, I try to avoid overspeeding any component of the action, so that my right wrist may still unhinge naturally once the downward weight shift is completed.

For me, this properly timed release of the right hand is crucial to the outcome of all short shots, in that it allows me to reflexively work the clubface back to the ball from a highly controlled three-quarter swing position at the top, while transmitting enough "whipping power" to the clubhead to send the ball the required distance. As long as I keep sliding my legs targetward through impact, my hands will lead the clubhead and will release naturally, making for a sharp, solid, descending hit.

Those, then, are the fundamental movements and subtle technical points of what I have always referred to as my short golf swing. To visually appreciate the action as a coordinated motion, study the special color sequence photographs. Your goal, as always in golf but more than ever with the short-irons, is to groove the action to the point where you are able to concentrate much less on *how* to hit the ball than on *where* to hit it.

INCREASING BACKSPIN

I'm not big on trying to put large amounts of backspin on the ball with the short-irons. One reason is that my normal shots, being high-flying, land pretty softly. Another is that, even for the experienced player, it's hard to predict how far a heavily spinning ball will back up once it hits the putting surface.

Sometimes, however, the situation demands putting extra "stuff" on the ball, particularly when playing an approach to a hard green from a tight lie, or when hitting to a normal green with a strong wind at one's back. In both those situations, and some others, the percentage shot is one that practically stops dead.

You might think hitting a "stop" shot is a sophisticated art only suited to top professionals. The truth is that it's comparatively easy for any golfer to get the ball to sit down "like a hound-dog in front of a fireplace," as a CBS television commentator once described a short-iron shot I hit during the Masters. Here's how.

Address: Encourage an exaggerated upright swing plane by playing the ball a little to the right of the midway point in your stance, which should be even narrower than normal for a short-iron shot. Also, set up very, very open. Next, weaken your hold on the club by moving both hands to your left so that the "V"s point toward your chin instead of midway between your chin and right shoulder. After checking that the clubface is square to your target, squeeze the handle a trifle more firmly with your left hand.

LONG SWING (face on view)

SHORT SWING (face on view)

continued

continued

continued

continued

LONG SWING (down target view)

SHORT SWING (down target view)

continued

continued

continued

continued

From short range, the percentage shot is often one that bounces once then "stops on a dime."

Backswing: Swing normally, following the line of your "open" feet, knees, hips, and shoulders. The exaggeratedly rearward ball placement will get the club moving up quickly, prompting the proper narrow swing arc.

Downswing: The firm, weak grip will automatically delay the release of your hands in the hitting area. That, along with the ball-back position, will produce impact before the blade quite squares itself to the ball, so that, as you trap the ball against the face, you impart very sharp left-to-right cutspin. The ball will start slightly left of the flag, fly high, float back toward the target, and, on landing, practically stop on a dime.

PART 3

THE SMALLER SWINGS

Chapter 6

PITCHING

I've always been impressed by the concert violinist's ability to produce such widely varying and consistently beautiful sounds. Sometimes, in listening to a great violinist, I could swear his instrument has fifty strings, not just four.

One reason a world-class violinist excites me so is that I can appreciate the enormous efforts behind his seemingly God-given talents. Another is that the creative approaches to our "arts" are surprisingly similar. The violinist has worked exceptionally hard to learn the knack of creating different sounds by altering the angle and speed of bow across strings. I've learned how to hit a wide variety of pitch shots by making many subtle changes in angle and speed of motion, chiefly through alterations to my setup and the pace of my swing.

I could write an entire book on all the types of pitch shots a golfer can be called upon to play during a typical round on a fine golf course. However, because I believe that the only way a person can master the finer points of pitching is through experimentation in practice and experience in play, I'm not going to do that. Rather, I'm going to give you the fundamental swing keys that I employ when playing, first, a basic pitch shot, then a basic pitch-and-run shot. All of my special situation short-game shots are essentially variations on these two types of pitching techniques. And we will, of course, be getting into many of those in later chapters about recovering from various kinds of trouble.

THE BASIC PITCH SHOT

I'm honored that many of my fellow professionals around the world recognize me as one of the game's best pitching-wedge players. At the root of my success is a special technique I developed all on my own as a boy, while trying to figure out how to delicately loft a ball a short distance and land it softly, first with a 3-iron, then, after my "old-reliable" was stolen, with a 5-iron.

As things turned out, it was a blessing that I lost my 3-iron, because a 5-iron is shorter and more lofted and therefore a little easier to swing and control. However, a 5-iron is still a full two and a half inches longer than a pitching-wedge, and also has twenty degrees less loft. So, even with this club, I had to really use my imagination to dream up techniques that allowed me to hit soft pitchlike shots.

Eventually, after much trial and error, I found I could do so by manipulating the club under the ball in an unorthodox fashion. Basically, I concentrated on staying well back on my right side throughout the downswing, while working my right hand *under* my left into and beyond the hitting area. All these years later, those two maneuvers still remain the foundation of my standard pitching-wedge technique. The chief advantage they offer is the ability to throw the blade fully under the ball at impact, which is what causes it to lay down softly once it lands on the putting surface. However, let's look at the technique in its entirety.

The Setup

I begin by positioning the ball forward in my stance, which ensures I get the full value of the loft of the clubface essential to producing softly hit, soft-landing shots. I spread my feet just slightly apart at the heels, with about 60 percent of my weight on my left side to help promote the steep plane of swing also necessary for height. My feet are set a little open, both to limit the amount of body turn I make on the backswing and help me more easily clear my left side as I start down to the ball, which is vital to keeping the clubface open through impact.

I set my hips and shoulders pretty much square to the target line at address, which encourages me to swing the club essentially on the same path I employ on full shots, which in turn promotes consistency or "repeatability." Finally, I hold the club lightly to promote fluid hand action, with my hands in line with the clubhead and the clubface dead square to my target.

The Backswing

The major focus points of my backswing are leaving my weight left while *dipping* my left shoulder downward in a kind of reverse pivot that automatically propels my arms and the club upward. As the club swings up in response to the dipping of the left shoulder, my upper body actually rocks a little toward the target. By the time my left shoulder has rotated under my chin and the club has reached the completion of its motion in a three-quarter-swing position, my right leg is firmly braced in a straight-up-and down position, preventing any swaying off the ball.

In playing a short, extra-soft pitch I'm like the violinist who has to make slight adjustments in his bow technique to produce new sounds. Keeping most of my weight on my left foot at address promotes a very slight reverse-pivoting of my body going back, which in turn allows me to stay well back on the shot through impact, which in turn again makes it easier and more natural to roll my right hand under my left, thereby throwing the big portion of the clubface under the ball, which lofts the ball high and lands it softly.

The Downswing

In trying for quick-stopping pitch shots, many of my fellow pros depend on a sharp, downward, hit-and-hold action of the left hand at impact to impart heavier-than-normal backspin on the ball. As I have discussed previously, I hardly ever want to produce excessive backspin on a regular pitch shot, preferring to hit the ball softly and high so that its elevation and steep descent produce only one soft bounce before it "dies" and rolls slowly to the pin.

To accomplish this, I trigger the downswing by gently rotating my knees toward the target, which has the effect of rocking my upper body away from it, or to my right, while at the same time pulling the club downward with my right hand. This mini-reverse-pivot, or falling back movement, allows me to stay well behind the ball, with my weight heavily on my right side. Also, by forcing my left shoulder upward, the action allows my left hand to pass the ball before I slide the clubface under it with my right hand.

If I failed to fall back, my shoulders, legs, and hips would all drive toward the target, in which case my left hand would be bound to lead the downswing. Furthermore, because I would also shift most of my weight to my left foot and thereby set up a leverage action, I'd hit the ball a very steeply descending blow, which is something I've always been dead set against doing. To me, hitting down hard to get the ball up high and land softly is unnatural, unless you're in deep rough and have no choice but to chop the ball out, or the fairway is so firm that sliding the club under the ball is impossible.

Any time a player hits down hard, he runs the risk of speeding up his tempo to the point of mishitting the shot. Worse yet, hitting down hard, given a clean strike, imparts heavy backspin, which makes the behavior of the ball on landing tough for even the finest of golfers to gauge. Greg Norman had that unfortunate experience in playing the final hole of the 1986 PGA Championship at Inverness. Greg put so much spin on his pitching-wedge approach that, after landing well past the hole, the ball spun back into thick fringe grass, leaving him little chance for the birdie he needed to tie after Bob Tway holed out from a greenside bunker.

IMAGINE A FLAGSTICK IN THE LANDING SPOT

A lot of golfers leave long pitch shots well short. If that's your problem, try programming the following visual key into your normal preswing routine. Picture a flagstick implanted in the ground at your interim landing spot—where you want the ball to pitch before rolling to the hole. Then aim at the *top* of the pole. You'll find that the ball gets well "up" to the hole every time.

WHAT WATER?

If you get anxious or tight when facing a pitch over water, try imagining that a friend is standing next to the flag, ready to catch the ball in a baseball glove. Or actually ask your caddie or playing partner to tend the flag. Either strategy greatly increases your depth perception for the shot, while forcing you to concentrate so hard on the target that you completely block out the water.

THE "UNDERHANDED" APPROACH

Hitting a short pitch shot with exactly the right force for the intended trajectory and distance is a technique that can only be learned by experience. However, a useful drill is imagining throwing a golf ball ***underhanded*** with your right hand—if that's your "feel" hand—to a spot short of the flag, before you actually play the shot. Then simply try to reproduce the weight and feel of that action with the wedge in your hands. You'll probably surprise yourself.

CHOKE THE CLUB FOR BETTER FEEL

On short pitches, such as when you're trying to float the ball over a bunker or to a tight pin placement, choke down on the club about an inch. This will enhance your feel for making the correct length of backswing.

PRACTICE WITH FRIENDS

Practicing alone is tops when working on mechanics. However, if you're looking to improve your feel and touch—in other words, your hand-eye coordination—hitting shots with friends and making small wagers on the outcome adds an element of competition that makes you concentrate harder and longer.

Ideally, practice pitch shots from different distances around a green, to various hole placements, so you can see how the ball bounces and rolls on a real putting surface. If your course lacks a short-game practice facility, try pitching into cardboard boxes set out in a field or your backyard.

THE PITCH-AND-RUN

The pitch-and-run, more than any other shot in my bag, has contributed most to my tournament successes around the world, and particularly to my 1979 and 1984 British Open victories.

The links courses on which this major championship is always played feature undulating greens that are very firm and fast-running, making it frequently impossible to hold them with a normal pitch shot. If the ball fails to land exactly on the perfect spot on the green, it can carom off a mound or severe slope and into a mass of greenside trouble. Consequently, for me, a low-flying shot that lands short of the pin—or short of the green if its surface is really hard, or I have a strong wind at my back and the entrance is clear—and rolls the rest of the way, is usually the obvious shot.

I might play the pitch-and-run from as close in as fifteen yards and from as far out as seventy-five yards, on any course where the situation dictates and conditions permit. Normally, I play the shot with a pitching-wedge, but from fifty to seventy-five yards out in the fairway I often go up as high as the 8-iron, in that a less lofted club allows me to make a very short, effortless swing and still get the ball all the way to the hole.

A run-up shot I played in the 1983 Suntory World Match-play Championship at the renowned Wentworth course south-west of London will stay in my memory for a long time. My opponent, Arnold Palmer, was one up coming to the par-five eighteenth. After we each had hit two shots, my ball sat fifty yards from the green, while Arnold's was virtually pin-high in an ideal position for him to get up and down for birdie. "Seve, you must *hole* this shot," I told myself, as I painted a mind-picture of an 8-iron run-up landing short of the green, bouncing gently, and rolling into the hole, which was cut in the rear portion of the putting surface. I did exactly what I'd visualized, eagling the hole and going on to win the match in a play-off.

Whenever possible, I prefer to use the pitch-and-run over the standard pitch, because the swing is shorter and made more with the arms than with the hands, which provides a little more margin for error in terms of both tempo and swing mechanics. For example, if I swing a trifle too hard in trying to pitch the ball all the way to a pin cut, say, on the top level of a two-tiered green, the ball would probably bounce long and into trouble, whereas a pitch-and-run hit a little too firmly in this same situation would, at worst, roll only to the back of the green.

In capsule form, the modern-day professional's usual method of playing the pitch-and-run is as follows. With the ball positioned back in an open stance and his weight set heavily left, he picks the clubhead up with both hands, then leads the blade into the ball principally with his left hand, hitting down with a sort of stunted, punching action. Some players—most notably, Lee Trevino—have this technique down to near perfection, and I certainly don't want to knock it. Nevertheless, it's not for me, chiefly because I think it produces too much backspin and not enough true roll.

As I've looked at films of the old "legends" of golf, I recognize that I am of their school in believing that the most effective way of playing the pitch-and-run lies in turning the clubface in an open-to-closed pattern through the ball. This puts a tiny amount of right-to-left spin on the ball, which creates a shot that holds its line nicely as it runs along the ground.

The Setup

To hit the "runner," I normally position the ball just behind the midway point in my stance, although in so doing I'm always cautious not to move the ball too far back, for fear both of hitting down too sharply on it and of making contact before the blade has time to square itself to the target at impact. I spread my feet about shoulder-width apart at the insides of the heels, and distribute my weight evenly toward the balls of both feet to promote a relatively flat swing plane. (Remember that taking a very narrow stance at address, with your weight over to your left, encourages a steep plane of swing.)

My alignment is square to my target line, chiefly for the personal comfort this body arrangement provides me. I stand a little more upright than usual, with my knees a little straighter to further encourage a slightly flatter swing plane. For the same reason, I normally grip the club close to the end of the shaft, and set my hands only slightly ahead of the ball. Normally, I aim the clubface a little to the right of the target to compensate for the touch of hookspin I impart on the ball, due to the open-to-closed swing I make.

The Backswing

Going back, I rotate my knees fairly briskly in a clockwise direction, which promotes a full weight shift to my right foot and encourages my arms to swing the club on a flattish plane. Also, I allow my head to move ever so slightly off the ball to the right, for I've found that a slight sway of my upper body on the backswing discourages an early wrist break and stops me from picking the club up too abruptly. (I would never normally advocate a body sway because of its weakening effect on the upper body coil, but in playing the pitch-and-run I'm not looking to generate power by winding my upper torso, as I must on bigger shots. My arm speed and the right-to-left spin I impart on the ball is what carries it to my landing spot and rolls it to the hole.) At their highest point in my backswing my hands are at waist level, the clubface is fanned open, and my right wrist is only slightly cocked.

The Downswing

Rotating my knees smoothly but smartly targetward while shifting weight back to my left foot triggers the downswing. I then have the feeling of effortlessly pulling the clubface back "to," then "along," the target line predominantly with my arms. And finally, through impact, my right hand rolls easily and smoothly over my left as my right shoulder moves nicely under my stationary chin.

On long pitch-and-run shots, a flatter swing arc, together with lively knee action on the downswing, encourages me to roll my right forearm over my left through impact, thereby imparting right-to-left spin to the ball.

FOCUS AT AN INTERIM SPOT

On all pitch-and-run shots, once you have carefully analyzed the situation and selected a landing spot, focus your attention *solely* on that spot—never on the pin. The more strongly you confirm to your mind the exact destination of the ball, the more likely you are to make the proper length and force of swing to hit it to the spot you picked.

STAND TALL TO PLAY THE PITCH-AND-RUN

The pitch-and-run swing I make is controlled predominantly with my arms. It is flatter because this type of arc better allows the clubface to move from square to open going back, then from open to slightly closed through the ball. This closing action of the clubface imparts hookspin to the ball, which allows me to make a slower and shorter—and thus a more controlled—swing and yet still get the ball to roll all the way to the hole.

Standing slightly *taller* to the ball encourages you to swing the club primarily with your arms and on the desired flatter plane.

CLASH A PAIR OF CYMBALS

Working the knees actively toward the target on the downswing increases your arm speed, promoting good acceleration of the club and thus crisp contact on long pitch-and-run shots.

To promote this lively lower-body action, imagine that you have a pair of musical cymbals attached to the inside of your knees, then try to clash them as you move freely through the impact zone.

DON'T BE PROUD ON WET GROUND

In playing a pitch-and-run off a wet fairway to a wet green, always take one more club than you otherwise would. That way you'll make a smooth swing—rather than a forceful one that could cause a fat shot—and automatically compensate for the slow surface you're hitting to by making the ball roll more.

Chapter 7

CHIPPING

I believe that chipping is one of my stronger suits. I think this is due primarily to the fact that, before I make my club selection or decide on the type of stroke I'm going to make, I am extremely careful in considering all of the variables—the lie of the ball, the distance to a landing spot, the topography between the ball and the hole, the speed of the putting surface, and, of course, the distance to the pin.

By contrast, many of my amateur playing partners invariably rely on only one favorite club and one kind of stroke to play all of their greenside shots. To me, that's about as intelligent as trying to catch trout and swordfish with the same tackle. Trying to hit a variety of short shots with one club is a very hard way to play, if only because it requires so much and such deft manipulation of the clubface with the hands. To do that correctly even some of the time, especially under the pressure of competition, demands extremely fine touch and feel, requiring constant practice. Therefore, I'm convinced most golfers will chip much more consistently by letting a variety of clubs do more of the work for them.

It's true that I play a lot of short shots with one club—the sand-wedge—but it's still not "the" chipping club for me, any more than any other single club in my bag. Even with the improvisational skills I learned as a boy with my trusty 3-iron and 5-iron, my present chipping arsenal includes the 4-, 6-, 8-, and 9-irons, as well as the pitching- and sand-wedges. The reason is that each of these clubs offers a particular amount of carry and roll without any manipulation on my part. Thus, once I've evaluated and ingrained the "powers" of each club, chipping becomes much more of a science than a guessing game. For example, I know that if I set the clubface of a 4-iron squarely behind a ball, then make a relatively short and wristless stroke, it will yield 10 percent "flight time" to 90 percent of "roll time." Similarly, my normal 6-iron chip flies 25 percent of the way to the hole; the 8-iron, 40 percent; the 9-iron, 50 percent; the pitching-wedge, 60 percent; and the sand-wedge, 75 percent.

My actual chipping technique is pretty basic. First, I select the *least lofted* club that will carry the ball to a preselected spot on the green, based on providing room for it to roll the remainder of the way to the hole. Second, the less lofted the club I choose, the shorter the stroke and the less physical effort I put into the shot. Third, the farther the ball is from the green, or the closer the pin is cut to the green's edge, the more lofted club I play.

I prefer to use an essentially wristless, pendulumlike, arm-swinging stroke to sweep the ball off the turf when it is sitting up nicely, the reason being that it's easier to control such shots predominantly with the arms and shoulders than with the hands, especially in a highly pressured situation. This type of swing produces a low-running shot, while a more wristy or handsy technique yields a more "floating" kind of shot that lands softer and sort of trickles rather than rolls smartly to the hole.

The setup and stroke I use to hit the "runner" varies sharply from my "floater" technique. Let's look at the particularities of each.

THE "RUNNER"

On a straightforward run-up chip from the fringe, I use a totally wristless stroke with the clubhead moving on as flat-bottomed an arc as I can achieve, my thinking being that the less the clubhead rises from the ground the more solidly it will meet the ball.

I position the ball midway between my feet, setting them about six inches apart at the insides of the heels. This narrow stance lets me feel like my entire body is closer to the ball, which increases my sense of being in complete control of the stroke. I use an open stance, pulling my left foot back a couple of inches from the square position, to give me a better picture of the line, and to provide clearance for my arms and the club to swing freely through the ball. My shoulders are set *square* to the target line, which promotes a virtually straight-back, straight-through swing path. My knees are slightly flexed and my weight is set mostly on my left side, where I try to keep it throughout the entire chipping motion.

Using my normal overlapping grip, I hold the club very firmly in both hands to discourage a loose, wristy action that could fly the ball too high with too much spin. Also, I grip down a couple of inches on the club for better control. I set the clubface square to the line on which I want the ball to start, keeping my hands a little ahead of the ball so that the clubshaft leans slightly toward the target. (If your hands are even with the ball when you set

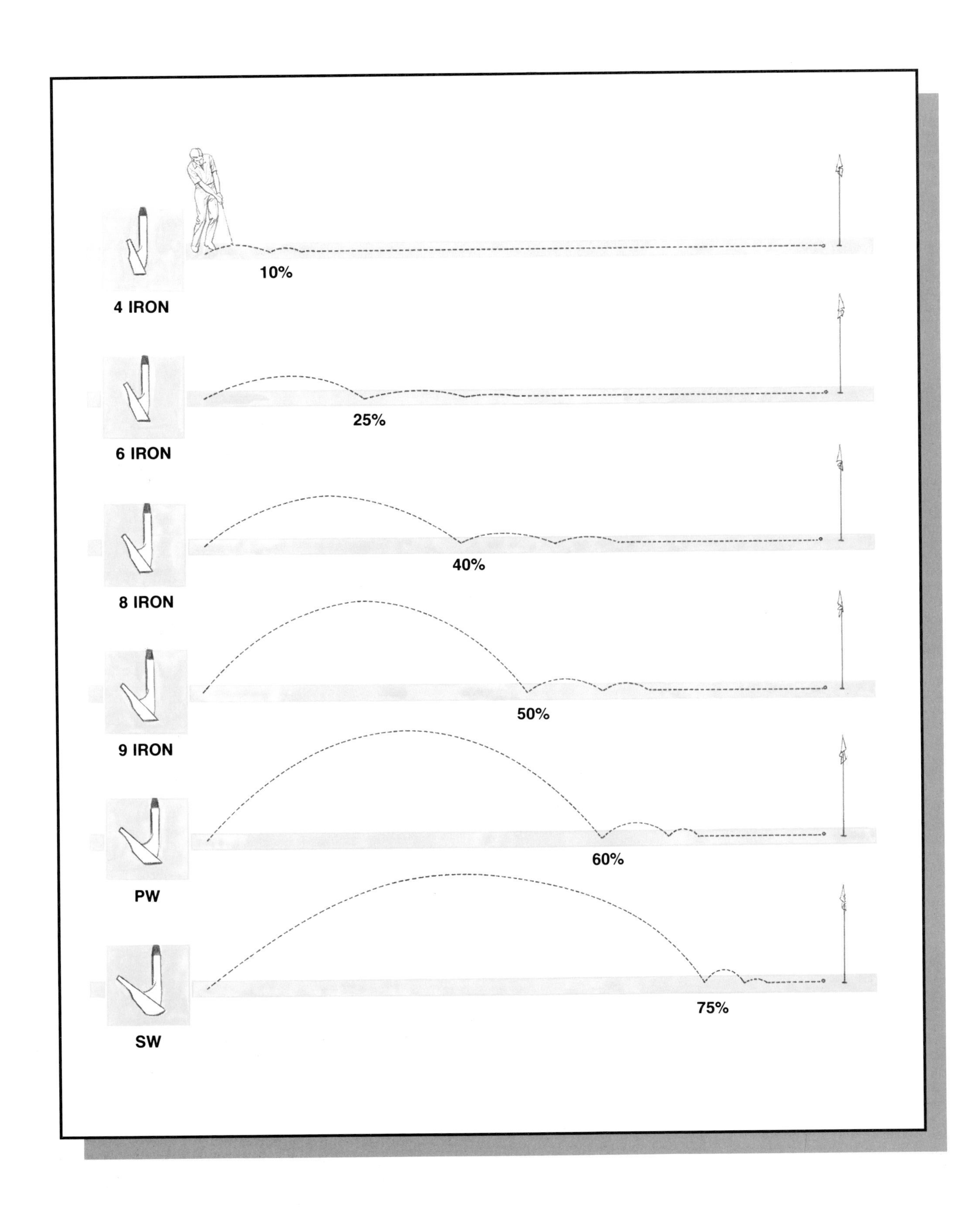

Want to chip better? Try keeping a copy of this flight-and-roll chart in your head.

A steady head on the backswing and "quiet" wrists throughout the entire action are keys to hitting the running chip.

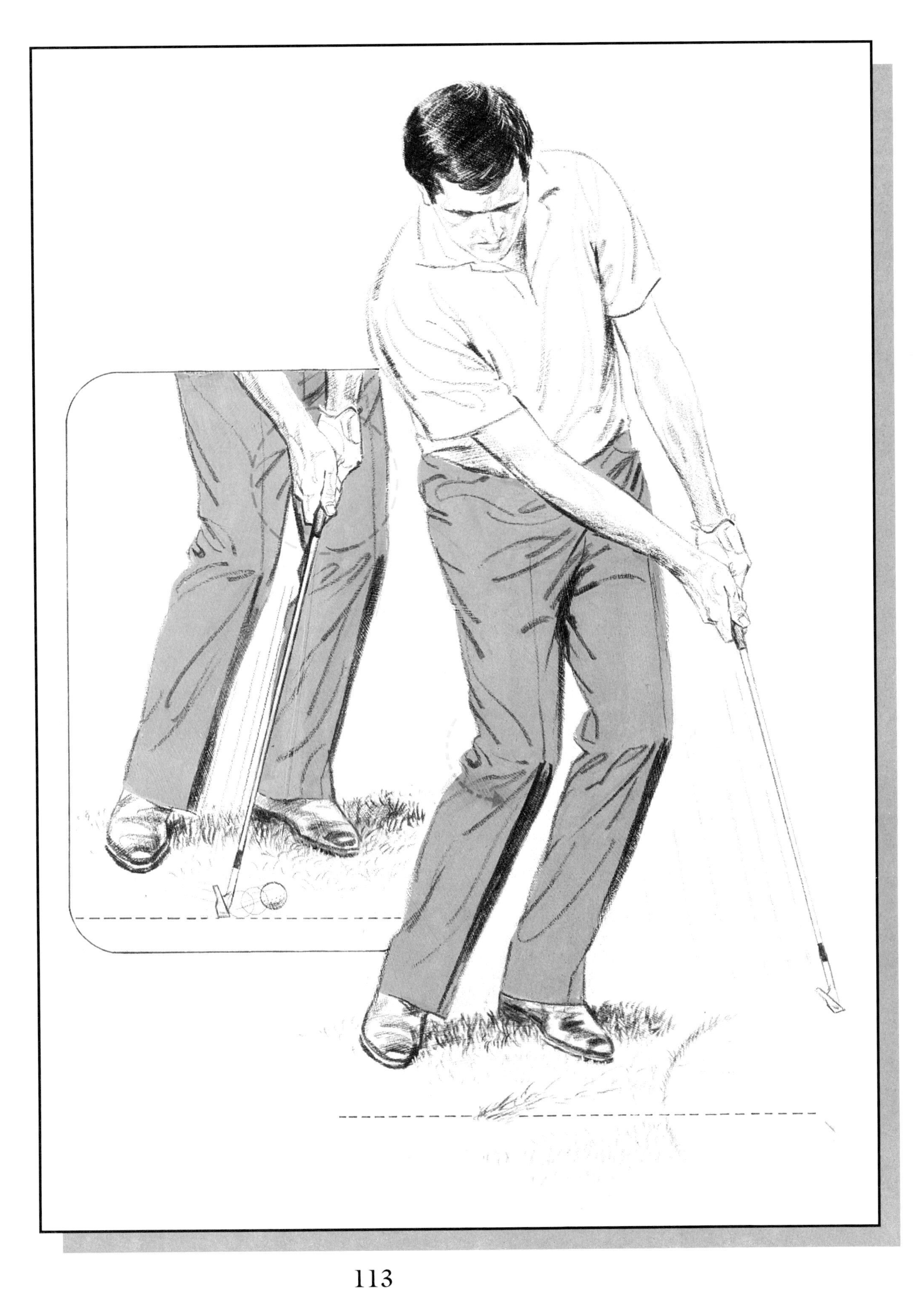

up to chip, they are likely to return to that relationship at impact, promoting a faulty scooping kind of action that results in much mishitting.)

It always makes sense in this game for a player to accommodate as many of his natural instincts as possible, thus I permit a very slight rotation of the knees and hips to prevent me from becoming overmechanical, while also enhancing the rhythm of the stroke. But I strive to keep my wrists almost entirely out of the action when I hit the runner, in order to reduce the chance of giving the shot that little extra "pop" at impact which could roll it well past the hole. Also, when your wrists hinge drastically on the backswing, you lift the club at a steep angle, which encourages hitting *down* instead of *through*, which in turn produces more height and backspin than you want on this shot.

Swinging the club back, I keep my head perfectly still, gently rotate my left knee inward, and pull the club virtually straight back along the target line with my right hand as far as I feel I need to relative to the length of the shot.

Coming down, I pull toward the target with my left hand to discourage my strong right hand from prematurely rolling the clubface closed, which would pull the ball left. Then I rotate my right knee targetward to help me crisply *brush* the clubhead through the ball along the target line. At impact, I try simply to return to my hands-ahead address position, which enables me to cleanly nip the ball off the grass just before the swing reaches the bottom of its arc.

THE "FLOATER"

The natural loft of a sand-wedge is usually enough to lift the ball from wiry greenside grass, or out of a relatively tight lie, but, using the above technique, it may give you too much roll when the pin is tightly located. Thus, in playing such shots, I want to put cutspin on the ball to land it both more softly and closer to the pin.

With the ball opposite my left heel, I take a comfortably narrow stance, in which my feet, hips, knees, and shoulders are aligned well left of the target. The forward ball position encourages me to stay well behind the shot at impact, which is the key to hitting a soft-landing shot. The open alignment promotes an out-to-in swing path that helps create left-to-right cutspin.

To avoid delofting the club at impact and hitting a low shot, I set up with my hands slightly behind the ball, and with a little more of my weight on my right side than on my left.

On the backswing, I pull the club up on a steep outside plane principally with my right hand. Then, leaving my weight heavily on my right side, I pull the club down, again principally with my right hand, while seeking the feeling of sliding the blade cleanly under the ball, the end result being that at impact, my hands are actually *behind* the ball.

I probably don't have to tell you that this technique is a lot more complicated—and therefore a lot more risky—than the one I use for the running chip. To hit the floater, which is very much a "manufactured" shot, I must work the club almost entirely with my hands. In contrast, the runner is a dead-handed "mechanical" shot in which I can let the club do the work for me while making essentially a simple to-and-fro arm-and-shoulders swing.

To be an expert around the greens, you really need both of these shots in your bag. The answer to obtaining them of course, is practice, and then more practice, and then even more practice.

TRY THIS NONRUSH ROUTINE

Most high-handicap golfers rush their preswing chipping routines, whereas good players take all the time necessary to thoroughly analyze the shot in order to be able to pick the proper club and the correct swing to *most easily* get the ball close to the hole.

Here's my step-by-step routine that obviates haste.

First, I stand by the ball and carefully examine the lie. Second, I stare at the hole until I get a complete "feel" for the distance. Third, I wait until I see a particular chipping stroke working well in my mind's eye before I match a club to it. Fourth, before I take the club I acquaint myself with the desired swinging action by allowing my right hand and arm to swing freely back and forth as I rehearse the "feel" I want to create during the upcoming stroke. Finally, I hold the club normally in both hands and test my planned technique with practice swings until I feel I've got it exactly right.

TRY THE REVERSE OVERLAP GRIP

Short chip shots are like well-stroked putts, except that they travel part of the distance in the air. Thus the basic strokes are similar in nature: essentially, a wristless action controlled by the arms and shoulders.

Because of those similarities, you might consider copying those tour pros who use the reverse overlap grip so popular for putting, in the belief that it gives them more feel for the shot. To do so, simply rest the index finger of your left hand between the little and ring fingers of your right—the "reverse" of the standard overlapping grip. This puts the right hand a little more in control of the stroke.

THE PROPER GRIP PRESSURE

More than anything else, grip pressure regulates the speed of the hands in every kind and size of golf swing. When the grip is light, the swing will be wristy or "handsy," and vice versa. Because the running chip is a ***dead-handed shot***, grip firmly to quiet your hands. Conversely, to hit a soft floater, grip the club lightly so your hands can work easily.

SNUGGLE CLOSE FOR BETTER CONTROL

Standing too far from the ball, and thus "reaching" for it, costs you control over both distance and direction on chip shots by disturbing your balance, creating tension, and making you swing so mechanically you lose feel for the stroke. Furthermore, the farther you are from the ball the flatter the arc of your swing, and the flatter the swing arc the harder it is to resquare the blade at impact.

To guard against overreaching, feel that you are "snuggling up to" the ball at address. First, grip down a couple of inches on the club. Second, move in close and assume a narrow and slightly open stance. Third, relax your arms and let them hang easily and naturally as you place the clubface squarely behind the ball. Fourth, flex your knees and bend forward at the hips a little more than normal.

STAY "FLEXED"

Coming out of your inclined or flexed posture at impact is as lethal as taking your eyes off the ball. By raising your body up, you lift your hands so that the clubhead clips only the top part of the ball. Settle into a balanced address position, then ***maintain*** your degree of waist bend and knee-flex well into the follow-through.

STABILIZE THE SWAY

Average players are inclined to move so far off the ball that they feel lost at the completion of the backstroke, then as a result flick the clubhead at the ball in a desperate effort to make some sort of contact. The usual result is a topped shot.

To prevent the big sway, build a backstop into your body motion simply by setting your right foot perpendicular to the target line.

USE YOUR PUTTER WHENEVER POSSIBLE

It takes an above-average chip to match an average putt. Thus you should chip only when you cannot use a putter—unless, of course, the "movie" that plays in your mind's eye tells you differently.

BEATING SLOPING LIES

When your downswing follows the slope of a downhill lie, the clubface is delofted at impact and the shot runs very low and "hot." The opposite is true of uphill lies; in swinging up the slope, you add loft to the club and produce a higher, shorter shot.

To compensate for these conditions, take a more lofted club when chipping downhill and a less lofted one when chipping uphill.

CHIPPING OFF A BARE LIE

When chipping from bare lies, many amateurs fear the club will bounce off the ground before it makes contact with the ball. As a result they try to "pick" the ball too cleanly, and frequently top the shot. The odds of a solid hit are much improved by taking a pitching-wedge and playing the ball back in your stance with your hands set well forward of the clubhead. This setup both encourages a descending blow and converts the effective loft of a pitching-wedge to that of an 8-iron. You hit down, and the ball pops up and rolls as true as a putt once it lands on the green. Also, because the wedge contains more mass in the head than the other irons, you can use a shorter stroke for the required distance, reducing the odds of mishitting the shot.

GETTING THE BALL "UP" WHEN IT'S "DOWN"

When the ball sits down, half-submerged in spongy fringe grass, and you have plenty of green to work with, try either of these high-percentage shots: 1. Take your putter and, making a short, steep, *wristy* stroke, hit down on the top rear quadrant of the ball. 2. Take your sand-wedge and, with a pendulumlike putting stroke, strike the ball *just above its equator* with the leading edge of the clubface. Either way, you'll put sufficient overspin on the ball to make it roll the full distance to the hole, even if it has to travel over some hairy fringe grass along the way.

PUSHERS AND PULLERS CHECK BALL POSITION

Both pulled and pushed chips can usually be traced to faulty ball position at address. Playing the ball too far forward causes you to set your hands drastically behind it, which tends to aim the clubface left of target. Unless you somehow manipulate it back on line, it usually then returns thus at impact and you pull the shot left.

The opposite fault causes the shot to fly and roll right of the target. In playing the ball too far back toward your right foot, you naturally place your hands way ahead of it, which can set the clubface in an "open" position (looking right of target), which alignment you then replicate at impact.

To iron out these faults, check that the ball at address is never farther forward than your left heel, or farther back than the middle of your stance.

VARY CLUBS FOR INCREASED FINESSE

Bare spots, thin or thick grass, slopes, fast or slow greens, different distances—each variation and combination of variations calls for a particular club choice. So I suggest again that you observe and calculate carefully before you automatically reach for your "favorite club." Once you've pretty much mastered the basic chip from the fringe, practice with different clubs off difficult lies until you learn by experience which works best in which situation.

BACKYARD PRACTICE

Using the wristless stroke, determine your average distance with each chipping club, then mark off the lengths in your backyard. Let the first target area be your landing spot for a sand-wedge, the second for the pitching-wedge, and so on. Practice hitting balls with an array of clubs until you can carry each shot to the right space with some consistency.

EXPERIENCE IS THE FINAL ANSWER

Since every player has his own personal tempo, there's no hard and fast rule that says a certain length of swing with a certain club will inevitably yield a certain distance. So you can never depend on a generalized rule of thumb in chipping: You just have to practice until you develop feel for the "air" and "roll" time produced by your personal pace and force of strike. This is really the only way to develop hand-eye coordination, plus the judgment to pick the correct club for each particular chip shot.

BALLESTEROS

Chapter 8

PUTTING

If you are already a golfer, I probably don't have to tell you that the seemingly ultra-simple act of stroking a 1.68-inch-diameter ball across a smooth green surface into a 4¼-inch-diameter hole involves not only a high degree of skill, but also a tremendous amount of luck.

I can pretty well predict how I'm going to play from tee-to-green after my pregame warm-up, but the fact is that, after a solid practice putting session, I often still don't have a clue as to whether my putter is going to be hot as a pistol or cold as ice out on the golf course. On some days I miss every single putt in practice and sink absolutely everything in play. Other times, I drain everything in practice, but in play hang them on the lip, bounce them out, roll them way by, or leave them pathetically short.

On my good days on the greens, I feel like I'm *willing* the ball into the cup. Then I'm so full of confidence that I let out the shaft on my tee shots and go dead for the flagsticks even when they're in the tightest corners of the greens. I can afford to play with a go-for-broke attitude, because, even if my drives miss the fairways or my approaches are way off-line, I'm sure my putter will always bail me out.

On my *bad* putting days, I feel such pressure to keep my drives in the fairways and knock my approaches stiff that I frequently start to try to "steer" these shots, and end up hitting everything *except* the short grass. On days like that, I fully understand why Gene Sarazen has so often petitioned for a bigger cup! I also get the urge to trade in my faithful Ping putter, and sometimes even to totally rebuild my stroke. But then I remind myself of one objective fact: Usually, *neither the putter nor the stroke is at fault.*

As an innovative consultant for America's *Golf* magazine, Dave Pelz, has shown, even when a robot strokes putts exactly the same way on exactly the same line on tournament-class greens, some of them do not drop, due to tiny imperfections in the surface of the green that influence the ball one way one time and another way the next. And, obviously, that's a sizable factor in why even the best putters among the pros make only about 18 percent of their putts between twelve and thirty feet. Gary Player is right to call this part of the game an "inexact science."

Regardless of statistics, however, I still believe that, the better my putting stroke, the better my chance of holing putts. Like most tour pros, I spend hours and hours on practice greens around the world, trying to groove my action while ever remaining alert to a new twist that may suddenly work wonders and boost or restore my confidence.

I witness many different putting styles as I compete around the world, and the interesting thing is how many of them work so well. For instance, Bernhard Langer putts cross-handed from inside twenty feet and conventionally from outside that distance, while Bruce Lietzke putts cross-handed all of the time. Corey Pavin's left hand practically covers his right hand on the handle of his putter, while Hubert Green uses a deep crouch, a widely split-handed grip, and an exaggerated follow-through. Payne Stewart stands tall at address and sets the putterhead in a heel-up position. Isao Aoki sets the putterhead in an even more exaggerated toe-up position than me. Mac O'Grady is a right-handed swinger but putts left-handed. Fuzzy Zoeller positions his hands low and well away from his body, while Ray Floyd sets his hands high and close-in to his belly. Andy North feels most comfortable setting his feet wide apart, while Calvin Peete likes to narrow his stance. Danny Edwards stares at the hole to putt, while most players focus on the back of the ball, some on its overall area, others on specific parts of it. Ben Crenshaw and I are *really* different here, in that we focus more on the putter blade than the ball. Johnny Miller is a "rap" or punch-type putter, while Fred Couples employs a very wristy method. Tom Watson uses the wristless, arms-and-shoulders-only action, while Jack Nicklaus and I employ a combination wrist-and-arm stroke.

The huge variety of styles of good and great putters is proof that putting is by far the most idiosyncratic part of the game of golf. There are some fundamentals common to all of the top professionals, and it won't hurt you to include them in your method. But never be afraid to add your own personal touch by listening to your instincts. Only in that way will you ever feel really comfortable and confident about your putts, which—if there are any true ones at all—are *the* keys to making more of them.

BEFORE THE STROKE

I start trying to read the slopes of greens when I'm about ten yards away from them, not least because—especially in late afternoon—it's easier to see the big undulations from about that

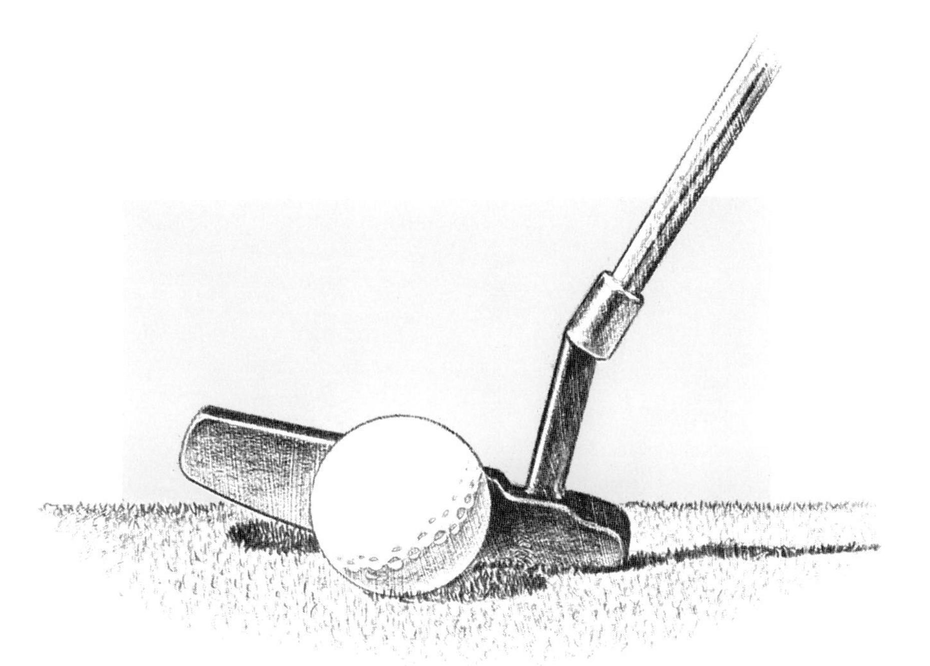

Half-soling the putter is an unusual feature of my setup. I do it because it feels comfortable and thereby enhances my confidence. Those are probably the two most important factors on the greens.

distance out. Then, as I mark and lift my ball, I glance at the line between it and the cup to get a preliminary feel for what I'll need to do.

Next, I walk around and check the line from both ends and both sides, to be sure I catch all of the lesser variations in ground contour I have to deal with. To get a bird's-eye view of the breaks, I look back to the ball from beyond the cup, then go back to a spot several feet behind the ball and make my final conclusions about break, grain, and speed, usually with the help of my caddie, as I look directly down the line.

At that point I start to swing my putter easily back and forth, with my right hand only, to begin to feel the weight of stroke necessary to roll the ball the required distance. Finally, as a boost to my confidence, I try to visualize the ball rolling across the green at the proper speed, on the correct line, and plopping sweetly into the center of the cup.

THE GRIP

It makes good sense to experiment with different ways of holding the club for putting until you discover the one that is both most comfortable and best allows you to consistently repeat *your* stroke. Compared to those two factors, the actual mechanics of the grip you come up with are relatively unimportant.

If you decide to try my combination arm-and-wrist stroke, then I think you will find that my grip, although it's a little unorthodox, will promote effective stroking of the ball. I've toyed with just about every putting grip imaginable, and have found that this one gives me the maximum sense of feel and control in my hands, which seem to me to be the top priorities in a putting grip.

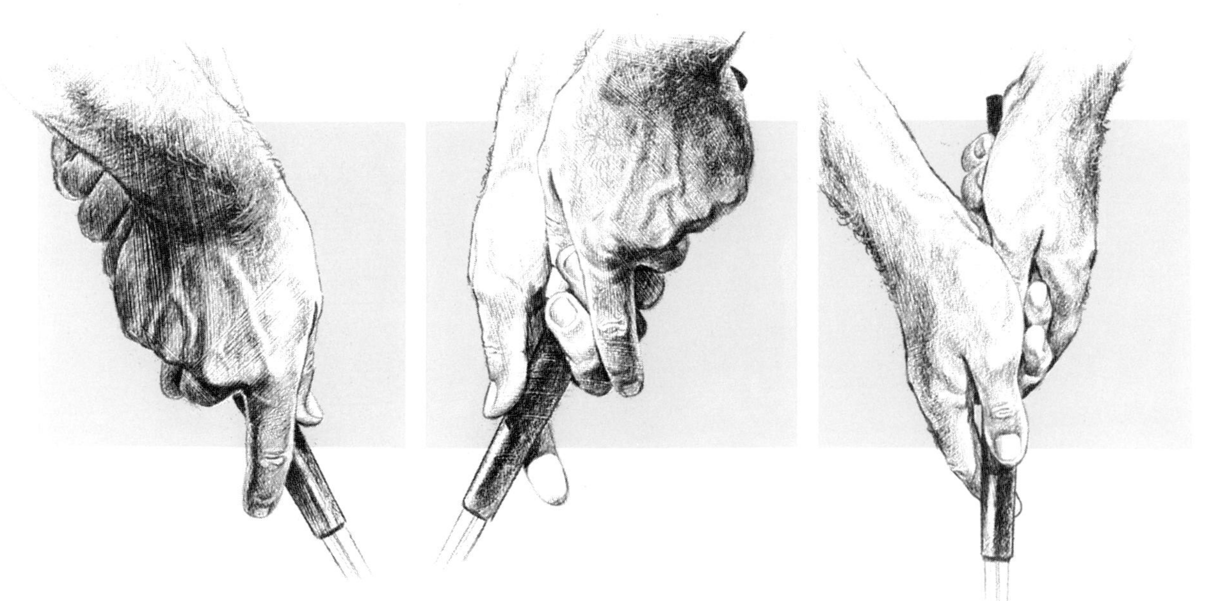

Draping the left forefinger mostly over the second and third fingers of the right hand and setting both thumbs straight down the shaft gives me the best "feel" for correctly guiding the putter blade back and through. Crooking the right forefinger under the club's grip induces heightened feel for controlling the distances of putts.

The highly popular reverse overlap putting grip works fine for most people, but in my case it inhibits the little bit of wrist action I depend on to control the speed of the putt. However, when I drape my left forefinger *downward* over the last three fingers of my right hand, I find I can employ just the right amount of wrist action while still keeping my left wrist firm enough to prevent it from overhinging as the blade swings through the ball.

In my putting grip, the back of my left hand and the palm of my right are square to my target line, just as in my full-swing grip: In other words, if a horizontal line were drawn straight through the back of my right hand and out the back of my left, it would be parallel, or square, to the starting line of the putt. I believe this position is crucial to good putting, in that a weak putting grip (one with the hands turned well to the left) tends to return the putterface to the ball in an open position, while a strong grip (hands turned well to the right) produces a closed face at impact. To promote a dead square alignment, I set both thumbs straight down the handle of the club.

I hold the club predominantly in the palm of my left hand, because I want that hand to act essentially as the fulcrum of the stroke. For the same reason, I look for a sense of firmness in the pressure of my left thumb on the shaft. With the right hand, I hold the club predominantly in the fingers, and with a lightness of pressure of the thumb against the shaft to promote more sensitivity of feel. As I stroke, the left hand simply guides the clubface, while the right hand pulls the putterhead gently back from and then pushes it smoothly through the ball.

An idiosyncrasy of my hold on the club is that I crook the tip of my right forefinger under the grip. I find this position to be critically important, because for me this finger is so sensitive that I use it to control the speed and distance of a putt as I push the putterhead through the ball.

THE SETUP

Many amateurs make the mistake of trying to precisely copy the putting setup of one or another of the tour pros. Accordingly, they rarely get into an address position that is really comfortable for them personally. You will never be a good putter for any length of time until you develop a setup that is comfortable for you, so always make a special effort in that direction as you work on this element of the game.

Experience has taught me that being truly comfortable must involve a readiness to continually make minor adjustments. Sometimes, for instance, the putter feels "long" in my hands, at which times I will choke down on the grip a little. At other times, getting comfortable requires switching from a slightly open to a dead square stance, or standing up a little straighter, or moving the ball back in my stance a little. The list of minor adjustments is almost endless, but here's the bottom line: *You won't be confident that you're going to hole the putt unless you are comfortable over the ball.* So don't be afraid to make small changes in your putting setup, from day to day, from hole to hole, or even from putt to putt. Many of the top players have done that throughout their careers and have putted better when it mattered as a result.

Such small personal variations apart, you are likely to become a better putter if you adhere to two key principles that almost every great stroker of the ball has incorporated into his setup.

The first absolute "must" is stable body position. Whether you stand tall to the ball like Ben Crenshaw, with your weight evenly balanced on the heels of both feet, or lean well over as I do, with most of your weight on the outside of the left foot, or pigeon-toed like Arnold Palmer in his prime, you *must* learn to stay very still in your body throughout the stroke by building stability into your setup. I guarantee that you will never see a golfer putt well with any kind of swaying or bobbing motion in his body.

I wish I had done a better job of taking my own advice on the short par putt I missed on the second play-off hole in the 1987 Masters against Larry Mize and Greg Norman. The ball was too far forward in my stance to be comfortable, and I made a mistake that many amateurs make: As I stroked the putt, I instinctively moved my head forward to get closer to the ball. That tiny movement was enough to turn my shoulders, arms, and the putter blade off-line, pulling the putt left. It was an extremely painful reminder that you have to be *100 percent comfortable* over the ball in order to maintain a stable body position during the stroke.

The second "must" is a positioning of the head that allows you to set your dominant eye directly over the ball—or, at least, set both eyes behind the ball but directly over the target line. Some trial and error on the practice green will tell you which position is most comfortable, while arranging you in the best position both to see the line to the hole and to align the clubface squarely to it.

Personally, when my eyes are directly over the ball—which I normally play opposite the inside of my left heel—I feel disoriented and uncomfortable. Furthermore, such positioning makes me concentrate too intently on the ball and not enough on the line it must take, producing a tendency to "jab" at the putt rather than letting the stroke flow with the proper gentle acceleration through impact.

Consequently, on short putts—inside say fifteen feet—I set my eyes a little behind the ball and directly over the target line, from where it's easier both to look along the line and to be able to square the putter blade to it. The latter is vitally important to me not only in terms of mechanics, but because I get a psychological boost from knowing I have taken "dead aim." Once I am sure the blade is correctly aligned, I feel so confident about holing the putt that I rarely am tempted to "peek" before contacting the ball.

On long putts, I'm a little unorthodox in my eye line, but for a good reason. The longer the putt, the more the putterhead naturally swings to the inside of the target line going back, and I want to be able to correct any mistakes in the direction of this longer backswing by manipulating the blade back on course with my right forefinger. I find it easier to use my peripheral vision to spot such a faulty movement of the blade when my eyes are a little *inside* the target line, rather than directly over it.

Obviously, this whole technique—eyes inside the line, watching the putterhead swing, manipulating it if I need to—has taken years of practice to assimilate, and it's not something I would recommend to the average play-for-fun golfer. However, if you're so bad a putter now that you feel you have nothing to lose by experimenting with watching the putterhead, be sure to set your head and eyes only slightly inside the target line. That's because, if they are too far inside, you'll "see" an erroneous line to the right of your target, and accordingly aim and stroke in that direction.

Regarding the stance, I normally set my feet a little less than shoulder-width apart, chiefly because that width seems natural and comfortable to me. Normally, too, I set up with my feet slightly open to the target, chiefly because I feel this gives me the clearest perspective of the line to the hole.

Even though my feet are open, I usually square up my shoulders and hips, chiefly because a square body alignment makes it easier to swing the putter back and forward on the proper path. Like most pros, I "hang" my left arm easily away from my body, while resting my right elbow on my hip. This "at-rest" position of my right elbow ensures that I swing the putterhead slightly inside on the backswing, while the free left elbow makes it easier to keep my left hand and arm moving smoothly toward the hole on the forward swing.

THE STROKE

My putting stroke is essentially predetermined by my setup. Once I feel ready to go, I trigger the backswing by gently pulling the club away from the ball with my right hand, after which my feeling of the stroking motion is essentially that it "just happens." I never feel as if I'm ever forcing any part of the stroke.

Like most good putters, I steady my head and swing the putter blade low to the ground, both going back and coming through.

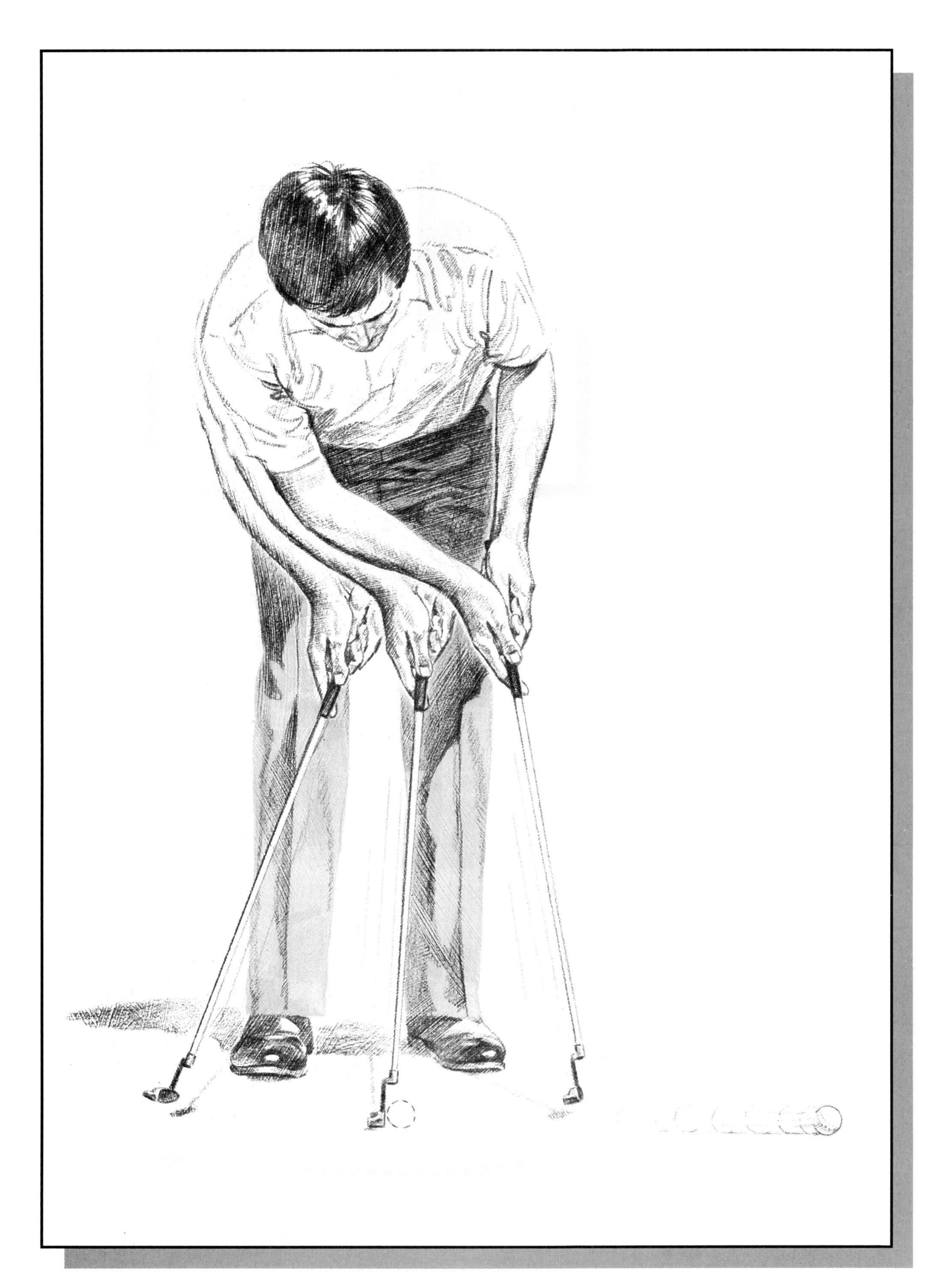

On the backswing, I try to swing the putterhead low to the ground and slightly inside the targetline. When I stay truly steady in my body as I swing back, while maintaining the "V" formed by my arms and shoulders at address, the stroke always comes off as I want it to.

On the forward stroke, my goal is simply to return the putterface squarely to the ball while traveling directly along my predetermined target line, with just enough acceleration to roll the ball the correct distance. When putting my best, I have the sense that my left hand definitely guides the blade through the ball. Keeping my left wrist fairly firm and the back of the hand square to the target line reinforces that feeling.

I use my right hand to apply force to the stroke, gently pushing the putterhead through and past the ball with the blade traveling low to the ground. The longer the putt, the more forceful the sense of pushing with my right hand. I never feel that one hand is dominant, but rather that each performs its distinct role in harmony with the other.

Golf is an elusive game in all respects, but nowhere more so than on the greens. Even the greatest putters vary far more in their success-failure ratio than in the other areas of shotmaking, and for that reason are forever seeking and searching and experimenting with both technique and tactics.

I've always been a leader of the pack in this regard, and expect to remain one for as long as I play golf. So, to conclude this chapter, I thought it might be helpful to briefly set down some of my discoveries along the way.

All of them won't help you all of the time, and some may never help you at all. However, I believe a number of them will definitely help you a good deal of the time. And that, friends, with the short stick in your hands, is really all that you realistically can hope for.

ACCELERATION

Acceleration in the putting stroke must be smooth and gradual. When I lose my tempo, when I find myself swinging too slowly on the backswing then too fast on the through-stroke, I key on taking the putter back on the count of "one," then through on the count of "two." I like to think of the movement—and the tempo—as being similar to the motion of the pendulum of a grandfather clock.

This drill helps me to overcome any tendency to start the through-stroke before I've completed the backstroke, while also enhancing a gentle acceleration of the clubhead. The product is a solid strike, pure roll, and consistent distance.

GRIP PRESSURE

Basically, light grip pressure enlivens the hands and wrists, while a firm grip deadens them. Thus, naturally wristy putters should hold the club lightly, whereas arms-and-shoulders putters should grip quite firmly.

Wrist-arm putters, like me, should hold the club fairly firmly in the left hand (with heavier pressure particularly on the thumb), and fairly lightly in the right hand (with lighter pressure on the thumb).

THE "SWEETSPOT"

Most modern putters feature a dot, line, or arrow that marks the club's sweetspot, while also sometimes providing an alignment aid. You should always try to contact the ball at that point, because doing so produces the purest roll.

If you use an old putter lacking a sweetspot mark, make your own by filing a thin groove in the top of the putterhead.

To locate the sweetspot, hold the putter lightly between your thumb and forefinger at the very top end of the grip, so that the club hangs easily with the blade at chest height and facing you. Now, with a pencil point or wooden tee, gently tap the putter at different points along its face. When you tap on the sweetspot the impact will feel solid and the blade will swing straight back and forward pendulum-style without twisting off-line. That's the place to put the groove.

STAYING LOW

If you have trouble swinging the putter blade low in the backswing, try setting it down two inches behind the ball at address and beginning the stroke from there. This adjustment often also makes it easier to start the blade back smoothly, which for me has always been a key to keeping it low and on line.

THE STROKE'S "GEOMETRY"

Many golfers believe that a putting stroke should be a straight-back, straight-through action. They are wrong.

The head of the club should move straight back on the target line for a very short distance, then travel naturally to the inside just as it does on any other kind of golf swing. Forcing the putter to go straight back all the way along the target line breeds tension in the hands and arms, while also causing the blade to rise sharply so that you chop down on the ball and mishit the putt.

So, to encourage a solid stroke and a pure roll, allow your putter blade to move ***naturally*** inside the target line on the backswing.

THE "SPLINT" DRILL

The average amateur's worst putting fault by far is allowing the left wrist to hinge or collapse targetward through impact, closing the clubface and pulling the ball left. It's particularly common on short "must" putts.

Here's a drill that will cure the problem.

"Splint" the lower portion of your left forearm and the back of your left hand with rubber bands and a flexible six-inch plastic ruler, then practice stroking putts from a variety of distances without bending the ruler.

Ingrain the firm-wristed feeling on the practice green, because it is against the rules to use such an aid on the course.

OVERCOMING THE "YIPS"

"Yipping" short putts can often be traced to over-concern with the degree of break, and consequently insufficient concentration on simply rolling the ball smoothly into the hole.

On putts of two feet and less, forget all about the break unless the green slopes very severely. Just pop the ball straight into the back of the cup.

To encourage a firm, accelerating stroke, pretend there's a miniature target just behind the hole.

You might find that visualizing a target *behind* the hole helps you become a better putter.

THE CAREFREE APPROACH

I know only one player, free-spirited Fred Couples, who believes that being carefree on the greens is more important than being confident. Instead of thinking, "I will make this putt," Couples says to himself, "If I make it, I make it. If I don't, I don't." A carefree outlook, he says, relieves the pressure.

Since Couples is one of the game's best putters, maybe his mental approach is worth a try.

PLUMB-BOBBING

When you find it exceptionally difficult to read a break, plumb-bobbing can sometimes help. Here's how you do it.

Stand with your body perpendicular to the horizon and hold your putter at arm's length in front of you with only your thumb and forefinger securing the top of the grip, letting gravity ensure that it hangs vertically. Cover the ball with the lower part of the shaft, then close your nondominant eye. If the shaft now appears to also cover the hole, the putt is straight. If the shaft appears to be to the left of the hole, the putt will break from left-to-right. If the shaft falls to the right of the hole, the putt will break from right-to-left.

JUDGING SPEED

Most amateurs are so "line conscious" that they pay insufficient attention to assessing and sensing the speed of putts. That's a serious mistake, because the speed of every breaking putt greatly influences its line.

If you have trouble judging speed, get into the habit of carefully inspecting the grass immediately encircling the hole. That area is usually much firmer than the rest of the green because it has been trodden so heavily, causing the ball to roll faster as it gets close to the cup. Always compute this factor into your "reading" process, especially on long putts.

READING GRAIN

Since grass grain—the direction in which the blades grow and lean—affects many putts, you need to know how to read it.

Crouch with the sun at your back and look closely at the grass between your ball and the hole. A shiny look tells you the grain is with you, thus the putt will run more readily. Dull grass means the grain is against you, thus the ball will roll slower.

SLOW GREENS

I believe a heavy putter promotes smoother and more solid striking on slow greens. However, if you're really attached to a light model, but have difficulty getting the ball up to the hole, try hitting the top half of the ball—deliberately catching it "thin"—to get some overspin on it.

FAST GREENS

It's extremely easy to lose feel and misjudge distance on exceedingly fast greens, even for top pros. If that's your trouble, try a light putter—or lighten the hit by contacting the ball more toward the toe of the putterface.

VERY FAST, VERY SLOW

On a downgrain, downhill putt on a lightning-fast green, pretend that the hole is two feet closer. This strategy encourages you to ease the ball to the hole, thereby still leaving yourself a "gimme" if you miss.

Conversely, when putting uphill against the grain on a slow green, promote an accelerating stroke by imagining that the hole is two feet beyond its actual location.

WET GREENS

On thoroughly soaked greens, allow for only about *half* as much break as under dry conditions.

WIND

Heavy wind can disturb your balance at address, thereby disrupting the timing and tempo of your putting stroke. It can also blow putts off-line, or influence their speed. So:

1. Improve your stability by spreading your feet wider apart and bending more at the knees. 2. Increase your control over the putter blade by choking down on the grip. 3. Improve the odds on solid contact by making a shorter, firmer stroke.

LAGGING LONG PUTTS

It takes much practice and experience to develop an instinctive feel for the amount of force necessary to reliably lag very long putts close to the hole. But here's a simple practice drill that will help you to focus more on distance than on the stroke itself, which is basic to successful lagging. Assume your normal putting stance, then turn your head and focus intently on the hole, then keep looking at the hole as you make your stroke.

Initially this drill will feel awkward, but after a few sessions your eyes will become more accurate in assessing distance and your brain better at telling your muscles exactly how much force to give the shot. After a while, the improved judgment will remain even when you look at the ball as you stroke.

SHORT PUTT DRILL

Here's my favorite drill to force myself both to concentrate intently and to ingrain my stroke.

I place five balls at one-foot intervals along a straight line extending from the hole, then sink the first ball, followed by the second, and so on until I've holed all five. Any time I miss, I have to start all over again.

INDOOR PRACTICE

Stories about tour players going back to their hotel rooms to practice putting are legion, including the one about Ben Hogan having to hit a chair leg one hundred times consecutively from four feet before he could go to sleep—one miss and he had to start all over again!

If you are an indoor carpet-practicer, aim at a tiny target about the size of a coin. When you play the course, the cup will look like a bucket.

PREGAME PRACTICE

Merely dropping a few balls on the practice green and rapping them one after another isn't going to do much for your putting game when you take it to the golf course.

I believe the best way to practice before a round is the way you putt on the course itself, with *one ball*, putting until you hole out rather than just knocking missed putts away. To me, this is the best way to rehearse the competitive "everything matters" mindset you will need on the course.

A COMMON ERROR

An error common to many poor putters is shoving the right shoulder outward at the start of the through-stroke. This produces an outside-in clubhead path, which pulls the ball left of the cup.

To overcome this fault, imagine you're trying to swing the putterhead into the hole by keeping it on the target line all the way to the completion of your follow-through. Also, concentrating on keeping the right hip still helps greatly in holding the shoulder back.

SHARPENING YOUR FOCUS

On very sunny days, glare can distort your depth perception, as can shadows from overhanging trees, causing you to misjudge both line and speed, even from short distances. When you encounter such conditions, ask someone to tend the flagstick. Having an object in the hole, and a person standing by it, brings everything into sharper focus.

PART 4

THE FINESSE SHOTS

Chapter 9

BUNKER PLAY

Most amateurs know that successful sand play involves a specialized setup and swing that are somehow different from those used when the ball is sitting up in the fairway. However, when the typical club golfer finds himself bunkered during a round, he will try to pick the ball out clean by "scooping" it up with the clubface, or pound the blade deep into the sand behind the ball in the hope thereby of violently "exploding" the ball from the sand.

Ineffective as such methods are, our happy hacker prefers to take his chances with them, probably because he thinks of the bunker shot as a pro's play that's just too complex for him to be able to copy.

The truth is, of course, that there is nothing at all complicated about the basic sand-shot technique. Indeed, my method caters to most people's natural instinct to lift the club at a steep angle in the backswing with an abrupt wrist cock, then to release the hands and wrists early coming down and through the hitting area. That's okay, just as long as your right hand works the clubhead *under* the ball, unlike a conventional shot in which the right hand rolls *over* the left. But we're getting ahead of ourselves.

The first requirement for good sand play is a club specially designed for that purpose—a sand-wedge. The key features of this club are a high degree of loft, plenty of head weight, and a flanged sole that descends below the leading edge of the clubface. The ample loft gets the ball up quickly; the extra weight reduces the effort needed to swing the club; and the flange, through its "bounce" effect, stops the club from digging too deeply and helps it slide through the sand just beneath the ball.

A good sand-wedge is specifically designed to lift the ball out of bunkers by skimming shallowly through the sand beneath it.

However, even when armed with a good sand-wedge, most amateurs still have serious problems with bunker play. They seem to feel an instant rush of panic the moment they see the ball land in sand, which creates tightness and a hurried swing—exactly the wrong way to play the shot. In addition, the Rules of Golf prohibit grounding the club in a hazard, and hovering the blade behind the ball without touching the sand feels pretty awkward for most less skilled players. Digging the feet firmly into the sand, one of the keys to playing this shot consistently well, also seems to go against the grain, as does opening the stance, swinging from outside-to-inside the target line, and hitting into the sand *behind* the ball rather than the ball itself.

The answers to all these "unnatural" moves lie in going into a bunker and simply making yourself execute them until success gradually eliminates your fearfulness of them. Pretty soon you'll begin to feel the clubhead slide easily under the ball and through the sand, and realize that the sand truly does lift the ball out quite effortlessly, once you begin to swing more or less in the prescribed manner. Then, as you become more confident, the fear will turn into fun. Like some of the tour pros, you may even reach the stage where you prefer playing a sand shot over other types of greenside recovery strokes.

Of course, to become this proficient requires mastering a wide variety of bunker shots, so it can never be an overnight process. The subtleties of sand play—like knowing precisely how much to open the clubface, how hard to swing in different sand textures, how "hotly" a ball will fly out of a buried lie—can only be mastered through much practice and long experience. Also, once you've grooved the simple fundamentals for recovering from the basic bunker lies, you will find yourself doing some experimenting on your own, as I've always done and always will in the constant search for improvement that so typifies the true golfing addict.

THE BASIC TECHNIQUE

The typical sand bunker with its relatively high front wall, or "lip," requires a floating shot that rises fast, lands softly, and rolls gently to the hole. The sand-wedge is almost always the ideal tool for the job, and the basic objective in using it is simply to *skim* the sand out from under the ball at just the right depth to send it the desired distance. In the latter regard, keep in mind that, because sand absorbs energy very rapidly, the more digging you do, the less effective the shot will be, unless the ball is badly buried.

An organized and disciplined preswing routine is as necessary in bunker play as it is to all other golf shots. I include in my routine a particularly thorough and patient rehearsal, *before* I step into the sand, of the exact swing that I intend to make, to the point of "seeing" the ball carrying the lip and rolling up close to or even into the hole. You should do the same.

In setting up to hit the shot, I position the ball opposite the inside edge of my left heel, while aligning my feet and body well to the left of the target line. The reason for this exaggeratedly open alignment is that it promotes an out-to-in swing that imparts cutspin to the ball; while the forward ball position establishes a skimming rather than a digging clubhead arc through impact. Both promote softness of landing, which is my ultimate goal on most such shots.

I refrain from setting the face of the club into its final alignment until I've carefully determined the sand's consistency by wiggling my feet firmly into it. This tells me two things: how much to open the blade, and the ideal point behind the ball at which the flange should make initial contact with the sand. Generally, the lighter the texture or consistency of the sand, the more I open the blade and the farther I hit behind the ball, in that the clubhead will more easily slide through the sand. When the sand is heavy, I reduce the opening of the clubface and move my contact spot nearer to the ball, because now I need more of a knifing than a slicing action through the sand.

In wriggling my feet firmly into the sand, I lower my hands an inch or two closer to the ball, so I compensate by choking down on the club an equivalent amount to guard against the blade digging too deeply at impact. Once I'm comfortably aligned and fully satisfied that my feet are securely planted, I grip the club lightly and set its face open—looking to the right of my target—the amount I feel is correct for the given conditions. My grip is light because a light grip encourages plenty of hand action, a key to playing this shot well. Setting the clubface open increases the "bounce" effect of the sole's flange and helps it ride more easily through the sand, while also allowing me to strike firmly with my right hand without any fear of closing the blade and thereby digging too deeply. Finally, in completing the address, I lean my weight to the left to promote an upright backswing, setting between 60 and 70 percent of it on that side and keeping it there throughout the swing. (If I have to play an extra-short explosion shot from a good lie, I like to keep my weight a little more centered to promote hitting against a firm left leg, which produces a higher and softer ball flight, so I favor the left side only slightly at address.)

On the backswing, I quickly cock my wrists as I pull the club up gently with my right hand. Because I leave most of my weight left, my body turn and leg action are minimal, so the club usually swings back no farther than the halfway position.

Coming down, I key on turning my right hand *under* my left, thereby ensuring that the flange slaps into and through the sand first—never the leading edge of the clubface. If I then simply maintain my hand speed and strive for a high finish, the action feels entirely effortless as the ball floats up and out on a cushion of sand and settles softly by the hole.

THE BURIED LIE

When the ball is anywhere from completely buried to sitting in a "fried-egg" lie it has to be truly exploded from the sand, and the starting point for doing that is to leave the sand-wedge in the bag and select the pitching-wedge instead. The reason is that the sharper leading edge and narrower flange of the pitching-wedge makes it much easier to knife its face deeply down into the sand beneath the ball.

Step two is to create a short, forceful, V-shaped golf swing. To do that at address I play the ball farther back in my stance—nearer the inside of my right heel—which promotes a very quick pick-up of the club in the backswing. Also, I set my feet, knees, hips, and shoulders relatively square to my target line, which promotes a more forceful blow by ensuring that I swing the club virtually straight up and straight down through the ball.

After squirming my feet into the sand, I further guarantee a steep or V-shaped swing and a sharply knifing blow by leaning my knees and hips targetward until I feel that at least 75 percent of my weight is on my left side. Finally, I square the clubface to the target and hold it over a spot close behind the ball. Normally, I set my hands only slightly in front of the ball, but when the sand is really firm I will move them even farther forward to promote even more of a descending blow and thus an even deeper cut. Usually, I choke down a little on the grip for greater control, and squeeze firmly enough with my hands to prevent any loose-wristedness in the swinging action.

I make the backswing for this shot by turning my left shoulder under my chin while keeping my weight left, my head almost perfectly still, my wrist action minimal, and my right elbow tucked in close to my hip to prevent the arc of the swing from flattening. Throughout the backswing I depend very little on pulling the club up with my hands; I rely more on the turning-under action of my left shoulder to swing it upward. Keeping my weight so much to the left naturally restricts my backswing, so that the clubhead usually swings no farther back than chest height.

On the downswing, I drive my hips and knees simultaneously targetward and downward, creating leverage that helps me forcefully accelerate the club with my hands and arms so that the blade descends very powerfully into the sand. Then, once contact is made about an inch behind the ball, exploding it out in a big shower of sand, the swing is over. On this shot, in other words, there is no follow-through, no attempt to finish high. All I do is just pound the clubface deep into the sand and leave it there.

A couple of years ago, Sandy Lyle, the 1985 British Open and 1988 Masters champion and one of the world's best bunker players, shared with me a mental image that I hope will help you as much in doing what I've just described as it did me.

To promote a steep swing, Sandy thinks of the action he uses to splash a friend who is standing close to him in a swimming pool. In other words, the right hand swings virtually straight up, then straight down, plunging into the water just as the clubhead must plunge deeply down into the sand.

Finally, in extra-wet or heavy sand, toe-in or hood the face of the pitching-wedge by setting your hands well forward of the ball. This adjustment helps to ensure that the club's leading edge meets the sand first and at a very steep angle, thus knifing the blade deep enough to get well below the ball and surely explode it out.

One last word about bunker shots. Spend enough time practicing in the sand so that you begin to feel at home there. Then, when you get in a bunker on the course, try to stay as cool and relaxed as if you had a perfect fairway lie. Calmly and deliberately *think* your way through your swing keys, then make the shot easily and without hurry.

BEATING FLUFFY SAND

To minimize "fat" shots in fluffy sand, try weakening your grip by turning both hands well to the left on the club's handle. This will help to keep the clubface open through impact, and thus enable it to slide more easily through the sand, rather than digging in.

PUT EGG ON THE FACE

A visual image that will help you better "splash" the ball from the sand is to imagine it as the yolk of an egg, with a small imaginary circle around it as the white. Swing to remove the *entire* egg from the sand and you'll be cooking!

TWO SAND-WEDGES

A deep-flanged sand-wedge will tend to skid or "bounce" too much off heavy or wet or coarse sand, often thereby producing a "thinned" shot. Conversely, a shallow-flanged sand-wedge tends to dig too deeply in light or dry or powdery sand, resulting in a "fat" shot that often remains in the bunker.

My suggestion, then, if you are a traveling golfer, is to own a sand-wedge of each type. That way, you can test each in the practice bunker before you play and carry the one that best meets the prevailing conditions.

HOW TO REHEARSE

If you touch the sand in a bunker with the clubhead before you take your swing, you incur a penalty. However, there is nothing to stop you making practice swings *outside* the bunker. To rehearse the type of sand shot you play most frequently, aim at a spot about two inches behind an imaginary ball, swing slowly and smoothly, and consciously roll your right hand *under* your left as you contact the turf with the flange of the club while being sure to follow-through fully. Get the feel of this two or three times, then step into the trap and match your practice swing.

LOOK AT THE SAND, NOT THE BALL

A common mistake of amateurs in bunkers is getting "ballbound"—focusing so intently on the ball that they become tense to the point of being unable to swing fluidly.

The strategy that best helps me stay loose is to consciously focus and keep my eyes on the point where I want the club to enter the sand, once I've assessed its consistency by wriggling in my feet. Incorporating this simple procedure into your bunker routine will give you a very specific target, instead of just a vague idea of where you want the flange to enter the sand, which will greatly improve your chances of delivering the club accurately. With practice, you'll learn where the contact spot should be, depending on the lie, the texture of the sand, and the length of the shot—remembering that, in general, the closer to the ball you strike the farther it will travel.

FROM FARTHER OUT

One of the game's most troublesome plays for the average golfer is the long greenside bunker shot. His tendency is either to try to pick the ball out cleanly and skull it, or swing so hard that the club sticks in the sand and the ball stays in the bunker or goes only part of the necessary distance.

The key to this shot is the proper setup. By standing a little farther than normal from the ball, with your feet spread slightly wider than your shoulders, you promote a relatively flat swing arc that allows you to take a very shallow cut of sand and send the ball flying all the way to the stick.

GO SLOW

Golfers instinctively swing overaggressively in sand because they feel the ball must be *forced* out. The result is that they either bury the blade in the sand and leave the ball there too, or skull the shot way over the green.

A relatively speedy tempo and hard hit is okay when you face a buried lie because you need force to get the clubface deep enough into the sand to cut beneath the ball. However, when the ball is "sitting pretty" and the shot is short, you should swing just about as slowly as you can without becoming wooden or jerky. This slow pace allows you to gently splash the ball from the sand so that it floats easily over the lip, lands on the green, spins from left to right, and just trickles down to the hole.

A slow-motion swing is bound to feel pretty foreign at first, but stay with it, because it's truly a key to good greenside bunker play. However, slow doesn't mean sloppy, so be doubly certain that you don't quit on the shot.

9-IRON TIME

Finding your ball buried in a steeply fronted fairway bunker some twenty-five to thirty-five yards from the green is not a pretty sight. However, you can hit the ball over the lip and onto the green, so long as you *don't* use a wedge.

Through experimenting I discovered that the 9-iron works wonders from this particular lie, principally because it has less loft and an even thinner flange than the pitching-wedge. Play the ball well back in your stance and make an extremely compact, forceful swing, driving the leading edge of the club down hard into the sand just behind the ball. Allow for lots of run.

THINK "FINISH HIGH"

The most valuable swing thought you can have before playing a normal twenty- to thirty-foot bunker shot is "finish high." This encourages you to accelerate the blade through the sand under the ball, rather than swinging back too far and quitting coming down—an almost certain way to leave the ball in the bunker.

ANGLED LIES

Two simple reminders for playing sand shots from severe slopes.

First, always play the ball opposite your *higher* foot. Second, make your downswing arc through the ball as *parallel* to the slope as you can, by setting your body at address perpendicular to the slope and keeping it that way throughout the swing. Vary your knee flexes to achieve perpendicularity.

In certain bunker situations, sometimes a 9-iron works better than a sand-wedge.

FLIGHT LINE

ABOVE AND BELOW THE BALL

When the ball is above your feet, aim the clubface right of the target to allow for a natural tendency to pull the ball left. Apply the opposite strategy when the ball is below your feet: Aim the clubface left to offset a tendency to push the ball right.

FAIRWAY BUNKER PLAY

Iron club and even fairway-wood shots from fairway bunkers can be played as easily as those off grass, so long as you maintain your normal swing tempo and make the following three adjustments that ensure hitting the ball before the club catches the sand.

First, establish a firm footing, but don't work your feet in so deeply that you lower your normal clubhead path to the point where you can't help digging into the sand before impact. Second, keep a little more weight on your left foot to encourage a steeper arc back and down, which further promotes catching the ball before the clubface touches the sand. Third, play the ball a little farther back than you normally would to promote delivering the clubhead just before it reaches the lowest point of its arc.

From hilly lies, aiming to one side of the green or the other is important, in that the sidespin imparted to the ball (almost unavoidable in such situations) makes the ball curve one way or the other.

CHIPPING FROM SAND

Given a good lie on wet and firm sand, plus a low front bunker lip, chipping the ball becomes a definite option for the reasonably skilled player. You can also sometimes chip from soft or powdery sand, provided the lie is good enough to let the clubface contact the ball cleanly.

To ensure clean, crisp contact, stay very still in your body as you swing the clubhead back low to the ground, using only enough arm and wrist action to promote good feel. Coming down, be sure to let your hands *lead* the blade into the back of the ball, because if the blade gets there first you will almost certainly leave the ball in the sand.

PUTTING FROM SAND

Putting from a greenside bunker can be a good call, provided the ball is sitting very cleanly atop the sand —preferably hard sand—and the forward lip is so low as to be almost nonexistent.

Most amateurs feel awkward playing this shot because the rules prevent them from resting the sole of the putter on the sand. I see this as a plus, in that slightly hovering the blade above the sand encourages me to hit the top half of the ball and thereby put overspin on it, which is what sends the ball scurrying through the sand and up to the hole.

Chapter 10

WIND PLAY

Every ambitious amateur knows that he is less than a complete golfer until he has learned how to keep his game together in the wind. A well-played shot into or across a stiff breeze is a thing of beauty, and the knowledge that you can hit such shots consistently well is a great confidence builder. Indeed, the skill to knock the ball down under the wind, and control its flight when playing downwind or crosswind, is what separates the great from the good—just watch what happens to otherwise capable players in wind-driven events like the British Open or some of the early-season tournaments in Florida. Fine wind play takes patience and perseverance, as well as complete knowledge of the necessary shotmaking techniques.

I began to learn how to master the wind when I was very young, largely by hitting shots on the beach bordering the Bay of Biscay, where the winds are always varying and often severe. Let me share my knowledge with you.

WIND AGAINST

Most amateurs are most fearful of stiff headwinds, because they are unfamiliar with the fundamentals for keeping the ball low. Their biggest mistake is swinging too fast and on too steep a plane, thereby hitting sharply downward and creating so much backspin that the ball actually flies higher instead of lower.

The key to a low, piercing shot is *powerful penetration*—swinging the club into the ball on a low trajectory to ensure an extremely solid strike, compressing it fully, and "chasing" it well into the follow-through. As is invariably the case in golf, it is the setup that predetermines this kind of strike.

As I prepare to play any shot into a headwind, I go through this simple checklist:

1. Square alignment—feet, knees, hips, and shoulders parallel to the target line.

2. Feet spread slightly wider than shoulder-width apart at the insides of the heels, to increase stability and promote good balance.

3. Majority of the weight on the left foot.

4. Hands set at least two inches ahead of the clubface.

However, for me the most crucial factor in setting up to hit a low, boring "wind-cheater" is the position of the ball relative to my feet at address. A popular theory is that the ball should be positioned no farther forward than the middle of the stance for a low shot, regardless of the club being played. To me, setting the ball way back promotes a straight-up, straight-down, over-steep swing that often produces a heavily backspinning shot that "balloons" high and weakly into the air.

As we've seen, I've never believed in one fixed ball position for any club. Every golfer's strength, suppleness, and swing tempo changes constantly, and it follows from this that his optimum ball position also changes from day to day. Certainly, everyone must have ball-position *boundaries* to work within, but, as we discussed earlier, these can only be found by experimentation on the practice tee. For low shots into headwinds, your goal is to find the boundaries that promote a low-to-the-ground *brushing* action of the clubhead, both on the takeaway and through impact.

Because it is even more essential that you make solid contact on the sweetspot of the clubface when playing into a headwind, another goal should be to keep your swing as simple and controlled as possible—slow but rhythmically powerful, in an arc that is short but wide. To create width of backswing arc turn your shoulders fully, but to keep the action compact minimize wrist action as you extend the clubhead well back along the target line with your arms. The ideal is a three-quarter-length swing, or even a little less than that with the arms, so long as you make a complete body turn.

Swinging down and through, keep your head very steady behind the ball, and your knees well flexed to help maintain balance and permit you to drive your legs toward the target as your hips uncoil, leading the clubface into the ball from well to the inside of the target line.

WIND BEHIND

Hitting a drive downwind is high on my list of favorite shots. However, as I've matured I've learned not to let myself become too greedy and try to hit the ball a country mile, which so often produces a wild swing and bad trouble. I also have learned to take an extra hard look at the hazards that normally would be out of reach on a calm day. Nowadays, if I have any chance of reaching a hazard that's normally out of my range, I gear down in club selection and play safely, by going with the 3-wood or a long iron, depending on the strength of the tailwind.

It is good advice with a strong wind behind you to tee the ball high and play it off your forward foot. Remember, however, that positioning the ball ahead of your left instep can cause you to top it.

In a light tailwind, I position the ball between my left instep and left heel, which is sufficiently far back to allow me to stay well behind it at impact, but sufficiently far forward for the club to make contact slightly on the upswing, provided that I:

1. Set up with 60 percent of my weight on my right foot;
2. Don't let my hands get ahead of the ball at address;
3. Make a free-flowing upright backswing with full body coiling;
4. Actively release my wrists in the downswing, by hitting hard with my right hand, while making sure not to roll it too quickly over my left through impact.

On approach shots, I make some drastic changes with a heavy wind behind me. With woods and long-irons, I will often purposely fade the ball with an out-to-in swing pattern to fly it higher and soften its landing. With the medium- and short-irons, I have two types of knockdown shots I play under the wind, depending on the pin position and the receptiveness of the green.

My techniques for both the "stop-shot," which sits down quickly, and the "go-shot," which runs, are really not that different. I play both with the ball well back in my stance and my hands well ahead of it, keeping my weight on my left side throughout the swing, which is no more than one-half to three-quarters, depending on the distance of the shot. The difference between the two types of shots is in the way I use my hands and wrists: very actively through impact, with the right hand turning over the left when I want the ball to roll; more passively with little rotation when I want plenty of stop.

CROSSWINDS

There are three basic ways to cope with crosswinds. The method you choose should depend on which you can most effectively execute after you've given all of them a fair trial.

The first method involves simply aiming off to the left or right and allowing the wind to blow the ball back to the target. The stronger the wind and the longer the shot, the more you aim off, of course. This is the easiest of the three crosswind methods to execute, and it's my recommendation for any golfer who hits reasonably straight but hasn't yet acquired the ability to "work" the ball reliably.

The second method involves favoring your dominant flight pattern. Suppose you're a habitual slicer confronted with a strong left-to-right crosswind. In addition to allowing for your natural slice, you must now aim even farther left to allow for the effect of the wind on the ball. Aim off the correct amount and the ball will ride the wind until it reaches the highest point in its trajectory, then drift nicely back to the target. However, because your slice is working with the wind, the shot will carry farther than on a still day, and you should allow for that by playing a more lofted club.

Leading the club to and through the ball with good leg action is key to hitting piercing shots that cheat headwinds.

"CHASE" BALL

In a right-to-left wind, your slice will be canceled out to some extent, so now you aim much less to the left of the target, if at all. Be aware, though, that, because your slice is working into the wind, you will obtain less distance, so use a stronger club.

Habitual hookers of the ball should simply reverse these instructions, working the ball into a left-to-right wind and aiming off and riding a right-to-left wind.

The third method is the one I use, but I believe it's really only suitable for pretty advanced players who have a strong affinity for "feel" shots. In a nutshell, the method consists of hitting a "punch-draw" into a left to-right crosswind, and a "punch-fade" into a right-to-left crosswind. The extra benefits are the way the ball firmly holds its line through being hard-driven "underneath" the wind, so to speak.

The Punch-Draw Technique

Assume a square address setup, and position the ball a little farther back than normal, permitting you to make contact while the clubface is looking squarely at the target but moving from inside to outside the target line, thus producing hookspin. Use *two* more clubs than normal for the distance at hand. Choke down on the grip, almost to the point of having your right index finger touching the metal part of the shaft, to give yourself maximum control of the club and therefore maximum control of the shot. As a final check, make sure the clubface is truly square to your target, because, with the ball back in your stance, it's very easy to unconsciously set the clubface looking to the right. Now make a compact, three-quarter-length backswing, with minimal wrist cock, and swing firmly through the ball with your hands and arms, being sure to go for maximum clubhead extension into the follow-through.

The Punch-Fade Technique

Again use *two* clubs more than normal, choke down on the grip, and position the ball a little back in your stance. This time, however, open up your stance and body alignment, to encourage you to swing the club outside the target line on the backswing and back across it on the downswing. Also, stand as close as you can to the ball without uncomfortably crowding it, because that will help you both to make a more upright backswing and to hit down more sharply on the ball.

The feeling you want going back is of swinging your hands, arms, and club up and away from your body. Swing the club back only to a three-quarter position, once again using very little if any wrist cock. From there, pull the club down across the target line principally with your arms, discouraging any premature rolling of the right hand over the left by gripping more firmly with the left.

This is a more difficult shot than the punch-draw because it forces you to counteract the natural tendency of the shoulders to turn, and of the body to swing the club from inside-to-outside. The shot also requires more physical strength and more practice, but, if you persevere, it will definitely save you some strokes in a hard right-to-left crosswind.

CHOKE DOWN

The very worst thing you can do when trying to keep the ball low into a headwind is to pick the club up sharply in the takeaway by being flippy-wristed. This narrows the arc, creating a steeply downward hit, imparting heavy backspin, and thus flying the ball too high.

Choking down slightly on the grip inhibits the action of the hands and wrists by reducing the club's swing weight, and thus will help you to avoid flippiness.

THE LONG-IRON "FLYER"

When confronted with a strong headwind, many amateurs who would hit the driver nicely to wide-open landing areas panic and try to steer the ball on narrow holes, usually to their disadvantage.

If you share this fear and fault, an alternative is the 1-iron—which is shorter and more lofted than a driver and therefore easier to control—purposely hit from a "flyer" lie to generate extra distance.

To create the flyer lie, dig the heel of your shoe into the ground and set the ball on the small mound that results so that a few blades of grass intervene between the ball and the clubface when you sole the club. Because of the grass intervening between ball and clubface at impact, which reduces backspin, the ball will fly lower and roll farther—in fact, it will often finish as far down the fairway as a solidly struck driver.

If you don't carry a 1-iron, play the shot with the longest iron in your bag.

CLUB SELECTION

Here's a rule of thumb for club selection in a headwind: For every 10 miles per hour of wind, take one more club. Thus, faced with a 150-yard approach, which would call for, say, the 7-iron in still conditions, in a 20 mph headwind your club becomes the 5-iron.

Chapter 11

OUT OF THE ROUGH

I still enjoy making the "heroic" recovery shot when absolutely vital, but I'm not the swashbuckler I was when I was younger. Maturity has bred a far greater awareness of how much "playing the percentages" contributes to winning at golf. Thus, when I confront a particularly poor lie in rough and it's obvious that the odds are heavily against me, I rarely try one of those "hit, hope, and pray" shots of old. Nowadays, I go for broke only when my back is hard against the wall and I absolutely have to have a birdie or an eagle to stay in the game.

Although I'm reasonably satisfied with my career accomplishments to date, I can get pretty upset with myself when I look back and realize the number and scale of shotmaking risks I routinely took in my early years as a tournament golfer. Yes, sometimes I pulled off the "impossible," which is how I got the reputation of being a shotmaking magician. But, overall, the hard fact is that my wild gambling hurt me more than it helped me. If I had started playing professionally with the analytical capabilities, shotmaking knowledge, and, most important of all, the self-control I have today, there would be a lot more trophies on display in my living room.

I started to become a much better tactician when experience finally became painful enough to convince me that sheer power was not the only answer to a golf ball in trouble. The result is that now when I land in the "junk," I carefully scrutinize the lie, figure a strategy by matching a club to the shot I see working best in my mind's eye, and stick to a feasible golf swing. I even have acquired the common sense—and, yes, the courage—to play an ultra-safe shot out sideways, or up the fairway to a place from where hopefully I can still salvage par with a well-played pitch and single putt. It is quite a turnaround from my early days, and, while maybe not as exciting, usually a great deal more profitable.

To me now, therefore, the rules for recovering from rough are relatively simple and straightforward—and in direct opposition to the habits of most club-level golfers. Frequently, for example, the high handicapper particularly will try to slug the ball with a wooden club from grass three or four inches tall, even when it's wet and lush, to a green that he probably couldn't reach from a perfect fairway lie. Or, sitting in heavy greenside grass, he attempts a shot even the pros have trouble with, and leaves the ball either right where it was or in worse shape. It all brings back memories of my own stupid mistakes that resulted in so many wasted strokes. Attempting a shot that is way beyond your capability, in a totally unrealistic attempt to "get well" with one swing, is the supreme sign of, at best, golfing immaturity and at worst sheer stupidity.

The good player who hits a shot in the rough accepts his fate emotionally on the basis that only he is to blame for the error, but that to err is human, then immediately begins applying his intellect to avoid compounding the error. In many golfing situations, plain common sense is far more important than being a shotmaking virtuoso: to really know what you can and cannot do with a particular club from a particular lie, and to resist the temptation of trying to do anything more.

I wish I could teach you how to master every trouble situation, but that's out of the question. Frequently, I discover some "new" kind of lie in the rough, and, even at my level, have to go back to the drawing board in order to figure it out. Furthermore, strength and swing styles differ greatly, both of which affect a person's ability to recover from bad rough. Nevertheless, there are several setup and swing fundamentals that apply to all golfers in trouble, and we'll look at them in what follows.

To put it mildly, despite my more serene approach to the game than in my younger days, I'm nowhere near as machinelike off the tee as I'd like to be, with the result that, during a typical tournament round, I play about 35 percent of my second shots from places other than the fairway. If I'm in light rough, apart from taking less club to compensate for the "flyer" effect—about another ten yards of distance due to grass intervening between the ball and clubface—I pretty much stick to my normal swing keys. However, when I'm trying to advance the ball up the fairway as far as possible from a very poor lie, or flying it to the green with "stop," I employ two very different techniques.

ADVANCING THE BALL LOW AND HOT

When the lie is so bad that the odds of getting home are truly unrealistic, I settle for a low-flying, fast-running, punch shot. This involves an upright backswing and a steeply descending hit, or "punch," that maximizes control of the shot by minimizing the club's contact with the grass through impact. In setting up, therefore, the top priority is to program steepness into my swing, which I do by a combination of positioning the ball farther back in my stance, aligning my feet open to the target line, and setting about 60 percent of my weight on my left foot. To avoid snagging the clubhead in the grass on the takeaway, I hover the club slightly above ground directly behind the ball, rather than soling it lightly as I normally do.

The common wisdom is that rough wraps itself around and slows down the hosel of an iron club, thereby closing the face through the ball. My own experience is that heavy grass tends to "grab" the toe of the clubhead and knock it back into an open position before impact. To compensate for this, I close the face at address very slightly in order to be sure that it will be square as it meets the ball. To encourage low flight and long roll, I also decrease the effective loft of the clubface by setting my hands a couple of inches ahead of the ball.

Once I'm fully satisfied that I have set up correctly, I picture the shot one last time, then trigger the backswing with what I can best describe as a stunted one-piece takeaway—a pulling of the club steeply upward with my right hand. Picking the club up thus restricts my shoulder and hip turn, which better allows me to make a controlled and compact three-quarter-length backswing. I try to be conscious throughout the backswing that much of my weight remains on my left foot, which is conducive to the sharp, punching-type blow I seek.

To trigger the downward motion, I move my legs laterally toward the target well ahead of my hands, which action reinforces the delofting of the blade at impact, thereby ensuring a low, running shot. As soon as my hips have started rotating targetward in response to the lateral leg movement, I pull with my left hand, seeking the feeling that my left arm leads the club sharply downward and does most of the work thereafter. However, photographs confirm that it is my right hand that finally whips the clubhead into the ball and supplies much of the punch at the moment of impact.

ADVANCING THE BALL HIGH AND SWEET

When the distance is such that I can go for the green from rough, height and stopping power become my key objectives. To promote them, in setting up I key on gripping lightly and positioning the ball well forward in an exaggeratedly open stance. The open alignment promotes a more upright out-to-in swing that imparts cutspin to the ball, while the forward ball position encourages me to keep my head and body well back through impact, which is critical to achieving height from my lie. The light grip is particularly important in that it promotes the loose, free-wristed swing and zippy clubhead release also necessary to maximize height.

Going back, I cock my wrists early and swing the club up steeply outside the target line, with, as usual, my right hand serving as the "pilot." Coming down, I key on keeping my head behind the ball with the majority of my weight heavily on my right side, both of which are promoted by minimizing my lower-

"Controlled power" is my mind-picture when I simply want to advance the ball from rough to a clear spot down the fairway. I improve my control by restricting the backswing, then attain power by whipping the club down and through the grass with my hands and arms while driving my legs targetward.

body action. I also try for a very free release of the clubhead with my wrists, allowing the blade to work well underneath the ball and fly it high. Obviously, some grass will come between ball and clubface at impact, which reduces backspin, but the idea is that the extra height makes up for the lesser backspin to soften the landing and stop the ball quickly.

I expect never to stop learning about golf in total, and definitely not about recovering from trouble. Here are a few other techniques I've discovered to date that will help you when you stray from the straight and narrow.

THE "FLYER" FACTOR

As we've explained, a "flyer" occurs when grass gets between ball and clubface at impact, increasing the distance the ball both travels through the air and runs along the ground by reducing the backspin it carries. Therefore, when choosing clubs for shots from rough, always remember to consider the flyer factor: Use more loft to compensate for the added carry and roll.

OUT SIDEWAYS IS SOMETIMES THE ONLY WAY

The average amateur seems to think there's a rule that requires him to go for the pin on every single shot, even when his ball is so deep in rough that he could hardly shift it with a bulldozer. Come *on*, now! When the lie is truly terrible, don't risk compounding a perhaps relatively minor mistake into a major scorecard disaster. Simply take a highly lofted club and play out sideways to the nearest short grass.

Here's the technique. Set up with the ball well back in your stance and your hands a couple of inches ahead of the clubface. Make a short, upright backswing with a free and early wrist cock, then pull the clubhead down sharply into the ball with your hands and arms. The ball will come out "hot," so allow for that by aiming at the widest or safest area of the fairway.

CLOSE THE CLUBFACE IN "JUNGLE" ROUGH

Out of curiosity, I once asked some amateurs why they opened the clubface when addressing shots from very deep rough. They told me they did so because an open face increases the club's loft, and they felt they needed added lift to extract the ball.

Well, as I indicated earlier, in my view opening the clubface simply makes the problem worse, because tall grass exerts drag on the club's toe end at impact, meaning that a player who opens the face to start with is likely to have it so open at impact that he risks shanking the ball.

To me, the proper technique for solid, accurate shots from "jungle" rough—*provided you hit down sharply*—is to set the clubface slightly closed. Now you can relax, because the toe-grabbing grass will drag the clubface into a square impact position.

FROM A PERCHED LIE

When the ball is perched really high on a clump of thick rough, almost as if it were sitting on a tee peg, the tendency is to hit up on the shot, the effect of which is to add about two clubs more loft to the one you're playing—an 8-iron turns into a pitching-wedge, for example. Consequently, you hit the shot much higher than you intend and lose considerable distance.

To deal with this lie, you can either take two more clubs than normal, or do what I do: Stick to the same club, make a short, compact swing, and key on *picking* the ball cleanly off the top of the grass—just as if you were hitting it off a tee.

FROM SANDY ROUGH

Most amateurs tend to hit long-iron and wood shots "fat" off sandy rough, the reason being an instinctive effort to get the ball up by driving the clubhead steeply downward into it.

What's needed instead is a shallow swing arc that promotes a *sweeping* action through impact. So, try for a more rounded or flatter backswing, a complete release of the clubhead into the hitting area, and a "chasing" of the ball with the clubhead well into the follow-through.

THE KEYS TO BERMUDA ROUGH

In the Bermuda-grass rough that's so common to courses in the southern U.S. and other warm areas, you need to take special care to make the cleanest possible contact, because the shot will fail if you hit the least bit behind the ball. The keys for clean contact are simple: 1. Set your hands ahead of the clubhead at address; 2. Pull the club up steeply with your right hand going back; 3. Keep your legs and hips moving ahead of your hands through impact; 4. Release fully with your right hand through impact.

AN ALTERNATIVE TO LONG-IRONS

The deeper the lie in rough, the less effective the long-irons become. Thick, tall grass snatches hold of their light, thin heads and twists the face one way or the other, making square clubface-to-ball contact almost impossible.

For that reason, I suggest you purchase a highly lofted, heavy-headed utility wood from your local pro. These modern purpose-built "recovery" clubs are heavily sole-weighted to help the head slide smoothly through thick grass and lift the ball up quickly, while still providing excellent distance.

GRASS GROWING TARGETWARD

The good news about grass that grows or leans *toward* the target is that it offers less resistance to the clubhead. The bad news is that it produces "flyers," making it very tricky to judge how fast the ball will come off the clubface, and thus how far it will fly and roll.

From such a lie, take one to two clubs less, depending on how much grass you think will intervene between ball and clubface at impact, then make your normal golf swing. Or, stick with the club required for the distance from a normal lie, but compensate for the flyer by swinging easily on a slightly out-to-in path and playing a soft fade.

GRASS GROWING AWAY FROM TARGET

When the grass is growing or leaning *away* from the target, it reduces clubhead speed and thus the distance the ball will carry. The answer here lies in selecting at least one more club than normal, then making an upright backswing from which you can drive the clubface down well under the ball, so that it rises fast and quickly clears the grass.

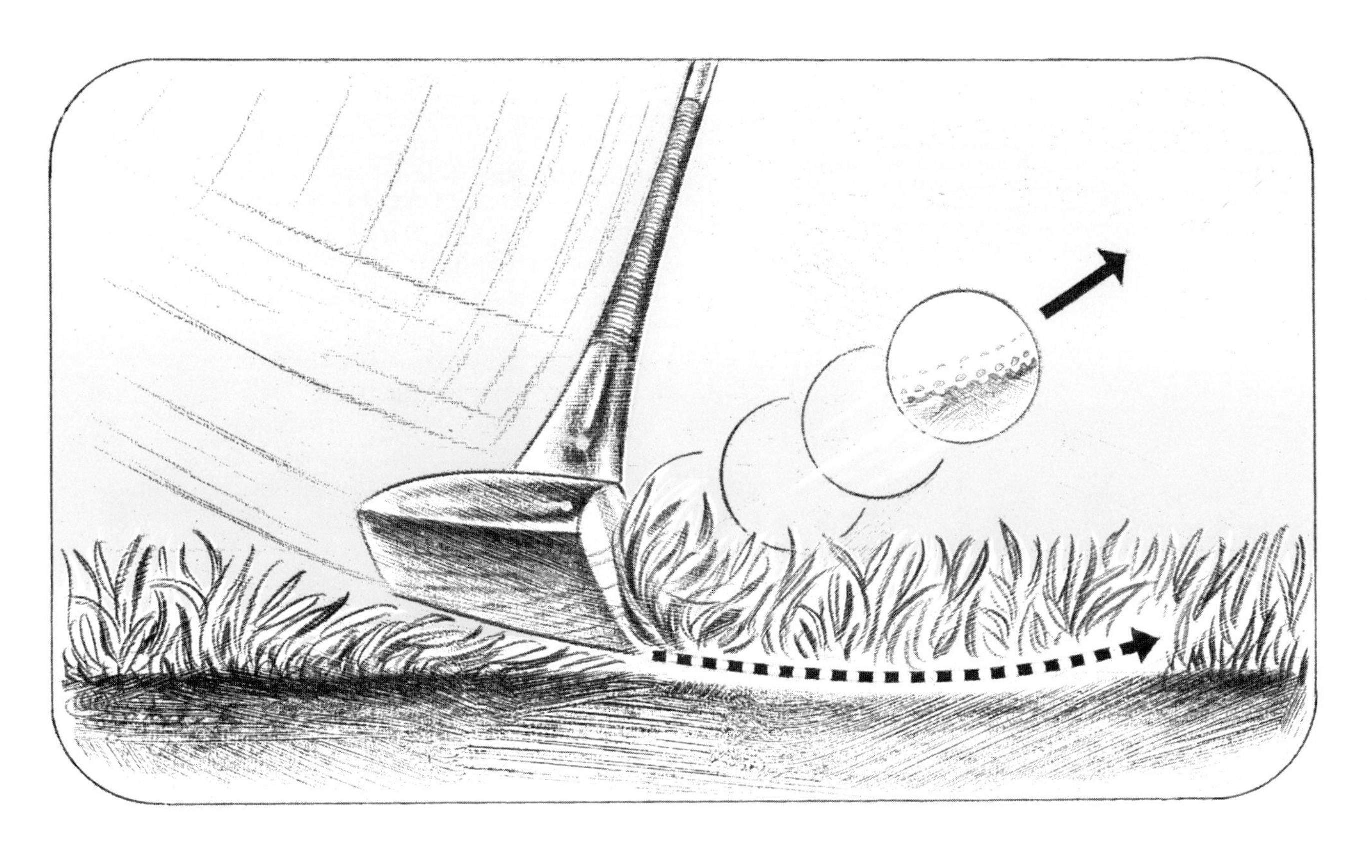

In thick or wet rough, a heavy-headed, highly lofted utility wood will easily get you more distance than a long-iron.

THE SOFT PITCH TO A TIGHT PIN

One of the scariest shots in golf is a short pitch from heavy greenside rough to a tight pin placement. By imagining you are playing the ball from sand, you can take a lot of the fear out of the situation.

Use your sand-wedge, open the clubface slightly, and play the shot just like an explosion from a greenside bunker. Going back, key on cocking your wrists early and making a short, upright swing. On the downswing, concentrate on contacting the grass about two inches behind the ball, then sliding the clubface under the ball with your right hand in control of the club but without letting it roll over your left. The entire movement should be gentle, to the point of almost feeling the weight of the clubhead simply dropping into the grass and then on under the ball.

This technique produces a shot that both flies and lands softly. As usual, some practice will tell you exactly how hard to swing for varying distances.

FROM AN UPHILL LIE

A short pitch from a grassy uphill slope may seem difficult because of the awkward footing, but it's relatively easy to pop the ball out and land it near the hole, provided you do the following:

1. Set your feet, knees, hips, and shoulders slightly left of the target line as you *lean into the slope*; 2. Grip down an inch or two on the club for extra control; 3. Close the clubface a hair to allow for the blade opening as it contacts the grass; 4. Swing your arms and the club back in one piece to knee-height by keeping your wrists firm and the majority of your weight on your left side; 5. Pull the clubhead smoothly down, and contact the grass as close behind the ball as you dare.

Off a grassy uphill slope, hit close behind the ball for the best results.

Chapter 12

OTHER RECOVERIES

There's an irony to the way I perceive, practice, and play the game of golf. I work very hard to groove a sound, repeatable swing, spending hours on the practice tee devising new shotmaking keys and drumming old ones into my muscle memory. During each session, as I strive to reach my full golfing potential, some part of me fantasizes about hitting every drive straight down the middle of the fairway, every approach shot stone dead, every birdie putt smack in the center of the cup. And yet, in my gut, I know this is all a pipe dream. The golf swing is simply not perfectable, which means that neither I nor anyone else will ever totally master what I consider to be the sport of sports. And, of course, if things were different and I knew I was going to hit every shot exactly according to plan, and that every bounce was going to go my way, I would probably give up the game because most of its mystery would have been lost.

Then, too, I genuinely enjoy the challenge of escaping from bad lies and other troublesome golfing situations. As a youngster, while improvising shots with my 3-iron, I would sometimes spend an entire day dreaming up some seemingly foolproof way of getting out of just one kind of awkward lie. When I would sneak with my caddie friends onto the Pedreña course just before sundown, we would designate the fairway of a particular hole "out of bounds," and compete to see who could play from the tee end of the rough to the green end in the fewest strokes. Consequently, many of the lies we encountered were extremely challenging, and, with precious pesetas at stake, we quickly became experts in improvisation. We also became pretty sharp at learning from each other's successes and failures, as well as from our own experimentation.

No matter what kind of game my friends and I invented, I always wanted very badly to win, and, for a lot of reasons, frequently did win. I was blessed with good coordination and a strong physique, I had good nerves, I was hungry to improve, and I had a wild imagination that allowed me to "see" shots vividly in my mind's eye, an art form further developed by my solitary one-club apprenticeship. Furthermore, I would fight hard to keep my mind from wandering to distracting thoughts, and consequently seemed able to concentrate more intensely than most of my friends. Every time I faced a particularly difficult shot, this intense concentration fired up my imagination, enabling me to picture the shot so well mentally that quickly my body could "feel" the swing improvisations necessary to execute it. Of course, I didn't always match the proper technique to the shot I had dreamed up, but even then the physical mistakes I made —like overdoing hand action—helped me to discover ever more new shots, rather as a chef stumbles on new recipes after accidentally messing up an existing one.

The more I practiced during those early days, the more I realized that the key to becoming a golfing Houdini is imagination, and that has remained the bedrock of all my recovery play. Nowadays, when in trouble, I always stand directly behind the ball, stare intently at my target, and wait patiently for the movies to begin. Sometimes I see so many shots come to life that I think I'm looking into a kaleidoscope. When that happens, I stay in the same spot as I rerun all the options until I "see" one working better than all of the others. Then, and only then, do I visualize the specific swing needed to execute the shot, and finally select the proper club for the task.

The high-handicap amateurs whom I so often partner in Pro-Ams tend to get angry anytime they miscue or get a bad bounce, then rush the recovery, compound the error, and end up with the ball in their pocket and their nerves rubbed raw.

I grew out of that stage many years ago. Nowadays, I don't blame the gods of golf for a bad swing, and I don't blame the course architect or greenkeeper for a bad bounce. I blame Seve Ballesteros, period. When I see a shot heading for trouble, I may get a little peeved, often to the point of letting my irritation show in my face. But I work off the steam while walking to the ball, and, by the time I reach it, am relaxed and ready to concentrate on determining and playing the best possible recovery shot. The more you can do the same, the more fun you'll have adding up your scorecard at the end of each round.

But enough preaching. Let me show you a couple dozen of the best ways to get yourself out of trouble.

THE WATER SHOT

There are times when you can and should play a recovery shot from water. My green-light situation is at least half of the ball being above water, plus the ability to obtain reasonably firm footing in taking my stance.

In playing this shot, you want the clubhead to *cut* through the water with as little resistance as possible. Thus the pitching-wedge, which features a sharp leading edge and plenty of loft, is the weapon of choice.

With the ball played back in your stance and your hands well ahead of it, make a short, steep backswing, then pull the club down hard into a spot close behind the ball, just as you would from a buried lie in sand.

Oh, and put on your waterproofs before you step up to the shot!

A pitching-wedge, a powerful downward hit, and unconcern about getting wet and muddy are keys to recovering from water.

ASSESS THE "PORTHOLES"

The phrase often used when a player gets lucky in the woods, that "Trees are 90 percent air," encourages the foolhardy to risk low-percentage shots out of tall timber. The gamble may pay off once in a while, but the odds are definitely not on your side.

In assessing tree-trouble situations, look closely at the branches and search for "portholes" to hit through—obviously, the bigger the better. If you are lucky enough to discover more than one possible escape path, mentally visualize a ball flying through each, decide which route is the *least risky*, then match a club and swing to the shot that played best in your mind's eye.

Obviously, if there is no clear path to thread the ball through, give up any thoughts of gambling and knock the ball back to the fairway as safely as possible, even if that means going sideways or rearward.

BEATING THE BUSH

An unplayable-lie penalty stroke and a drop clear is sometimes the only answer to a trouble situation, but don't settle for it until you've carefully weighed the situation and stretched your imagination about recovery possibilities. In doing so, remind yourself that you don't always have to remain on your feet to swing.

It frustrates me to see a golfer taking a drop from under a bush, when I'm sure he could have gotten the ball out quite easily by playing off his knees. Kneeling down often gives you sufficient room to swing the club without interference from the bush's overhanging branches to at least knock the ball back into the fairway.

In setting up for this shot, your hands will naturally be near the ground, with the clubshaft close to horizontal and the clubface almost vertical. Spread your knees comfortably wide, stretch out both arms in a relaxed fashion, and turn the toe of the clubhead in a little, closing the face to better insure solid contact with the ball. Lock your hips to promote a more lively arm swing, then on the backswing also lock your wrists to encourage a low takeaway and a flat arc. Coming down, uncoil your shoulders smoothly while swinging your arms freely through to "sweep" the ball off the grass.

Hitting from your knees can often save you a penalty stroke.

DISTANCE FROM A DIVOT

Utility woods—the 5-, 6-, 7-, and even the 8-wood—feature contoured soles, lots of loft, and plenty of head weight, thus are perfect for digging the ball out of shallow divots while still sending it a good distance. Just adhere to these two simple swing keys:

1. Set up open and lean 70 percent of your weight left to promote an exceptionally steep backswing.

2. On the downswing, keep the clubhead moving aggressively down and through to the target by pulling hard with both hands.

PINE NEEDLES

Pine needles are slippery, so in playing from them be sure to clear patches under your feet to get yourself firmly anchored. Pine needles are also loosely knitted together in such a way that the slightest touch with the clubhead can cause the ball to move. Consequently, I suggest you hover the clubhead above the ground at address to minimize the risk of incurring a penalty stroke. Position your hands ahead of the ball with most of your weight set left, then make an upright backswing and hit down sharply with your hands leading the clubhead through impact.

In playing from pine needles, hover the club above ground when setting up to guard against incurring an extra stroke by inadvertently moving the ball as you address it.

THE CAROM SHOT

When the ball is sitting so close to a tree trunk that you can't face the target and still make a normal swing, don't automatically decide that the best escape is to chip out away from the target, or to drop clear and take an unplayable-lie penalty. You may be able to bounce the ball off the tree and "bank it" onto the green, billiards-style.

To play the shot, face the tree with your entire body aligned to the left of its trunk—that way you avoid getting hit with the ball after it rebounds. With a medium-iron, make a slow, short, upright backswing, then swing the club down into the back of the ball using a "hit-and-hold" action of the hands at impact to stunt the follow-through.

Obviously, this is a shot that must be practiced if you hope to be able to accurately gauge the strengths of swing necessary on the course to reach the green from various distances.

Billiards-style golf can be a good strategy when blocked by a tree.

BALL IN DEEP DIVOT

Try my method of playing short to medium approach shots from fairway divots.

Set up open, with the ball played forward in your stance. On the backswing, purposely swing the club well outside the target line, then, coming down, use a lateral slide of the legs to make the arc more shallow as you cut across the ball from outside to in. The result is a high fade that sits down softly on the green, so be sure to compensate by taking at least one more club.

THE SOUTHPAW SWING

The left-handed shot for right-handers is a real desperation play, but, reasonably well executed, it can save you shots when an obstacle prevents you from taking a normal setup and making a regular swing.

Reverse your hand positions on the grip end of a lofted club, and turn the club over so that the toe faces down and is in position to contact the ball. Next, take enough practice swings to gain at least a little feel for the action. Then, settling for the easiest, most direct route, just swing instinctively but as short and smoothly as you comfortably can. The ball will fly sharply left off the angled clubface, so allow for that in your aim.

When the lie is so poor even a successful "southpaw" swing won't really do much for your score, it's much smarter to accept a penalty stroke and drop the ball clear.

FROM CLOVER

The key to playing shots from clover is to remember not to sweep the ball, because that type of action mashes the plant's leaves between clubface and ball at impact, creating an uncontrollable "flyer." Instead, you need to hit sharply down on the ball, which requires playing it back in your stance a couple of inches, setting and keeping your weight more on your left side, and cocking your wrists quickly in the backswing.

No matter how precisely you swing, some clover is bound to intervene between clubface and ball at impact, so compensate for the "hot" flight by selecting at least one less club than you would play from a normal lie.

THE "BUMP" SHOT

The delicate little pitch from a close lie to a tight pin placement over a steep bank or mound is one of the hardest and scariest shots in golf. If you don't feel confident about it, an alternative play is to bump the ball into the bank, from where it will hop and run the rest of the way to the hole.

Begin by trying to visualize the behavior of the ball through carefully studying the terrain. If the ground is soft and the grass lengthy, you'll have to hit harder or carry the ball to a higher spot on the bank, or both. If the ground is medium firm and the grass not too long, a good rule of thumb is to carry the ball about two-thirds of the way up the bank, so that it takes, say, two bounces before clearing the top. When the ground is very firm and the grass sparse, play the ball to skip most of the way up the bank, using a middle-iron instead of a more lofted club.

Because you always want the shot to fly very low, you should play the ball back in your stance with your hands ahead of it, making a short, firm-wristed arm swing that keeps the clubhead low to the ground both going back and following through.

Take the time to practice this shot occasionally from different distances with different clubs. Once you've hit a match-winner, you'll know the effort was well worthwhile.

HARDPAN

Trying to scoop the ball is the most common fault of the average golfer when playing from hardpan. As a result, his left wrist collapses through impact and his right hand involuntarily flicks the leading edge of the clubface into the top of the ball.

Don't make this shot unnecessarily complex. Set up to let the club do the work for you. So long as you position your hands ahead of the ball at address, then keep them leading the clubface through impact, you'll make crisp contact using your regular golf swing.

As the clubface tends to open as its sole contacts the hard ground, it's not a bad idea to compensate at address by toeing it in a hair.

THE SAND-RUNNER

Your ball is pin-high to one side of a fast-running green, but there's a shallow trap between you and the hole and you have very little putting surface to work with. You know that a regular pitch shot would finish well past the hole. What to do?

The answer is run the ball through the trap so that it reaches the green with just enough speed to roll to the hole.

The choice of club for this shot depends almost entirely on the texture of the sand. If it's soft, play a 7-iron and plan to carry the shot over most of the bunker, so that it touches down only once before it skips onto the green. With firm sand, take a less lofted club—say the 5-iron—and hit a low-flying shot that makes a series of short hops through the trap before skipping onto the green and trickling to the hole.

The technique is the same as for a normal chip shot: Essentially the stroke is wristless, with the hands always ahead of the clubface up to and through impact. However, if the sand is particularly soft, to the point that you fear the ball will stop in it, roll your right hand over your left a little more quickly through impact, thereby shutting the blade and imparting a little hook-spin to the ball.

TWO WAYS FROM SANDY LIES

There are essentially two ways of getting the ball close to the hole from a sandy, sparsely grassed greenside area.

When the ball is pretty much level with the putting surface you're playing to, and there's plenty of green to work with, the best strategy is a running chip played with a medium-iron. However, a raised green and a tight pin placement virtually forces you to try a high, soft-landing ball, so the percentage play is the bunker-type explosion shot. Chances are the sand will be firmer or coarser than the kind normally found in bunkers, so only slightly open the blade of the sand-wedge at address, then make a smooth, compact backswing and hit down hard about an inch behind the ball. The ball will pop up sharply and sit down quickly when it lands.

HEATHER

Most dedicated golfers seem eventually to find their way to Scotland, where the game evolved if it didn't actually begin. You'll enjoy the courses there even more if you know how to deal with heather, a wiry-textured, purple-flowered, wild-growing plant that snarls around the necks of golf clubs and closes down their faces like nothing else on the planet.

Unless you're extremely lucky and the ball perches high in the upper branches of heather, forget playing any kind of aggressive shot. Just reach for your pitching-wedge, identify the shortest route back to the fairway, then try the following:

1. Position the ball well back in an open stance.
2. Grip the club very firmly with both hands.
3. Lay the clubface open but don't ground it behind the ball. (Heather is very springy stuff, so the slightest touch with the clubhead could move the ball and cost you a stroke.)
4. Set 70 percent of your weight on your left foot and keep it there.
5. Make an unhurried, steeply up-and-down, *V-shaped* swing, and consciously lead the clubhead sharply down into the back of the ball with your hands.

Good luck!

BELLY THE BALL

Occasionally, the ball will stop on the manicured fringe but resting tight against the next, taller cut of grass around the green. This lie normally perplexes the inexpert golfer, who wants to use his putter but knows he will probably mishit the shot by snagging the grass behind the ball on the backswing.

Here's the answer. Choke down on your sand-wedge and set its leading edge level with the ball's equator. Moving your hands well down on the grip promotes control, while holding the blade above the ground allows you to swing the clubhead back with no hindrance from the high grass.

Keep your lower body very still, make a dead-handed, firm-wristed stroke, and try to catch the ball at or slightly above its equator with the bottom of the flange to set it rolling just like a putt. Be warned that it takes practice and good nerves to master this shot, so, if you're lacking either, remember that the margin for error between "too thin" and "too fat" is very narrow.

SOGGY GRASS

In hitting a shot off wet grass, you need to clip the ball cleanly, otherwise you'll take too deep a divot and lose both distance and accuracy. To encourage an accurate strike, take one more club than normal so that you don't press. To insure that you sweep the ball up at impact, play it a little more forward in your stance.

SHORT BUT HIGH

The short high shot over, say, a tree close in front of you is not as hard as it may appear.

You need to hit this shot as softly as possible so that it sits down quickly on the green. Start by aligning open, with the ball positioned opposite your left instep (aiming left of target encourages an upright swing, while the forward ball position helps you stay well back and "under" the shot). Set most of your weight to the right and keep it there. Use your sand-wedge and grip it more lightly than normal, which allows your hands and wrists to rotate freely and promotes the long, slow, loose swing that you need here. Finally, sense how much height you need relative to forward trajectory and open the clubface accordingly (practice will tell you this).

The key to this shot is setting and keeping your weight almost entirely on your right side throughout the swing, which puts your hands behind the ball at impact for even more loft.

Going back, allow the momentum of the clubhead to easily and fully cock your wrists early in the swing. Coming down, control the action with your hands and arms, being sure to strive for a complete release of the clubhead and a high finish.

THE LOW SHOT

When you must keep the ball low, as when escaping from under branches, your first consideration is club selection. This is where the 2-, 3-, and 4-irons come in handy. The lower the branches, the lower-numbered club you should select, provided the lie is reasonably good.

Choke down on the club, thereby reducing the width of your arc, which will help you to keep the ball down. Position the ball back far enough in your stance so that your hands are set well ahead of it, and put most of your weight on your left foot.

Going back, key on leaving your weight left while making a firm, compact, three-quarter-length swing. Coming down, consciously try to swing the grip end of the club through the impact zone ahead of the head, thereby delofting and slightly hooding the face to insure a very low shot. Allow for the ball to fly low and then run very "hotly" once it touches down.

THE DRAW

Being able to draw shots from right to left at will allows you to curve the ball around doglegs or other obstacles, as well as increasing your distance overall from tee to green.

As a youngster, I played the draw by assuming a strong grip, taking a closed stance, swinging on a flat plane, and rolling my right hand quickly over my left through impact. Since then I've learned that this is the hard way to draw the ball. Here's the *easy* way.

Set your feet, hips, and shoulders parallel to the line on which you want the ball to start, with the clubface aligned *square to your final target*—in other words, *closed* in relation to the line on which you start your ball. The more drawspin you want to impart to the ball, the farther right you set your body and the more you close the clubface.

Having set up thus, all you have to do is swing normally, and the ball will start to the right and draw nicely back to your target.

Keep in mind that right-to-left spin makes the ball fly lower through the air and run farther on landing, so take that into account in your club selection.

CLUBFACE

THE FADE

The ability to fade the ball from left to right at will is basic to good golf, particularly in terms of the extra height and softer landing obtained. In aligning your body, pretend that you're setting up to hit an imaginary target located slightly left of your actual target, but aim the leading edge of the clubface at your true target. Also, grip a little more firmly than normal with your left hand and a little easier with your right hand. This will encourage your left hand to lead the clubhead into the ball while reducing the tendency for your right hand to roll the clubface closed at impact. Otherwise, swing normally.

Because you swing along the path established by your body alignment, the club travels on an out-to-in path, starting the ball to the left of your target. However, because the clubface is open in relation to the swing path, left-to-right sidespin is imparted that curves the ball gently back to the target.

As the ball will fly higher and stop faster, consider taking more club than normal.

"Working" the ball at will is an art worth learning.

UPHILL LIE

An upslope increases the club's natural loft, causing you to hit the ball higher and shorter. Accordingly, be sure to select at least one more club, depending on the severity of the slope.

The sloping ground also presents you with a balance problem. Resolve it by tilting your body to your right at address, so that you stand as perpendicularly to the slope as you comfortably can, thereby giving yourself in effect a level lie. To prevent your body from swaying down the slope in the backswing, straighten your right leg and brace your right foot firmly at ninety degrees to the target line, while bending your left knee more than you normally would.

From this setup, your hip action will necessarily be somewhat restricted, which is fine because the entire swing should be made largely with the hands and arms to help with the balance problem.

DOWNHILL LIE

A downhill lie delofts the clubface at impact, so in principle always take less club on such shots.

Set your body perpendicular to the slope, and, because falling forward is your biggest danger, put most of your weight on your back foot at address, then keep it there throughout the swing.

On the backswing, minimize body motion for better balance, but be free with your hands, wrists, and arms in swinging the club back on an upright plane. Coming down, key on maintaining your knee flex, and, because it's so easy to top the ball when you're swinging downhill, make a real effort to stay with the shot by *chasing* the ball with the clubhead well into the follow-through.

On uphill lies, the hands and arms rather than the legs should play the more active role in the swing.

BALL ABOVE FEET

When the ball is above your feet you'll naturally make a flatter backswing, and your right hand will tend to overpower your left in the hitting area, both of which result in right-to-left flight. Allow for that by aiming the clubface and your body to the right of your target as you set up—the farther to the right the more severe the slope. Also, stand taller at address, which will better match your swing plane to the contour of the slope. Guard against losing your balance and falling back by distributing your weight equally toward the toes of both feet.

Once you're satisfied your setup is correct, think of making a smooth, compact swing while visualizing sweeping the ball away rather than digging at it.

BALL BELOW FEET

When the ball is lower than your feet, it will tend to fly from left to right, chiefly because the slope forces you to make an exaggeratedly upright swing and gives you insufficient mobility to get your hips out of the way for your right hand to swing freely through and square the clubface at impact. Allow for the fade by aiming your body and the clubface left of the target. Also, get down fully to the ball by widening your stance, bending at the knees, and holding the club at the very end of the grip.

Your backswing will be restricted but that's a plus, because a shorter and more controlled backswing is desirable on these difficult shots. Pull the club down with your hands on the forward swing, while being absolutely sure to keep the knee flex you established at address, otherwise you're likely to "stand up" and skull the shot.

Never try for too much on such shots, especially when the slope is severe.

When the ball is above your feet, you can figure it will fly left—the more so the higher the ball.

FINAL TARGET
INITIAL TARGET
STAND TALLER
WEIGHT ON TOES

PART 5

BEYOND MECHANICS

Chapter 13

PRACTICING RIGHT

Practice is a very personal aspect of golf, thus routines vary greatly from golfer to golfer. Nonetheless, most of the better ones agree on the objectives of the preround session. Above all, of course, we want it to loosen up our muscles and put our minds into gear for the game. The rest mostly has to do with achieving the desired feels in swinging both the short and the long clubs, and for pacing the little shots—the pitches, chips, and putts—to the hole.

What is not so simple is spelling out the exact nature of post-round practice. Mine can, and usually does, change drastically from day to day, depending on my mood, the course I'm playing, and the condition of my full swing and short game. Frequently, I will just work on such basics as synchronizing my right-hand and hip triggers, or on grooving good tempo. At other times I might spend a couple of hours honing a single full shot, practicing a specific aspect of my short game, or patching up a fault in my technique by "freezing" a correct position over and over again.

Let's take a closer look at these procedures.

PREROUND PRACTICE

I'm very careful never to make big swings without loosening up thoroughly first for fear of seriously straining a muscle, particularly in my back. Thus I begin each session by working the driver through my elbows so that its shaft lies across the middle of my back, then carefully stretching by rotating my upper body left and right. Next, I'll take two or three irons together and swing them slowly back and forth a number of times with a ten-finger grip.

I start my actual ball-hitting warm-up by playing lazy half shots with the sand-wedge, gradually working up to a longer and slightly faster swing by hitting a few balls with every second iron in my bag, from where I move on to the 3-wood and finally to the driver. By taking everything slow and easy, my timing (the sequence of the actions comprising the swing) and tempo (the speed of the overall swing) begin to blend so that, by the time I complete this part of the warm-up, my full swing is hopefully totally cohesive and coordinated.

I might add that, these days, I never finish off by hitting a string of tee shots at full throttle, a lesson I learned the hard way on the final day of the 1976 British Open at Royal Birkdale. I was nineteen years old at the time, and was leading Johnny Miller by two shots going into the last eighteen holes. When I got to the practice tee prior to the round, a huge crowd of spectators, writers, and photographers had gathered to take a look at the new "boy wonder." I still remember the "Ooohs" and "Aaahs" as I pounded out one enormous drive after another. It was great for my ego, but I was too inexperienced to realize that with every mighty swat my swing tempo was getting faster and faster. Even if I had, it probably would not have bothered me then, because I seemed so "in the rhythm" that my timing appeared perfect. I nailed about twenty drives in succession, dead on the sweetspot, and that's what fooled me into thinking I was swinging superbly.

Once I got on the golf course, it was a completely different story. I just could not get back to my normal playing rhythm, which is slower due to the need to show courtesy to playing partners. Also, during competition I must give myself time to fully plan shots, and to relax in my "bubble" between them. On that occasion, taking the fast practice pace to the course badly affected my play. In fact, I turned into the proverbial "basket case." I just couldn't find the swing tempo that had worked so well the previous three days. Due to my stupidity on the practice tee, everything was happening much, much quicker than normal, throwing off both my rhythm and my timing. Off the tee, I played what my friends on the U.S. Tour call "army golf"—left, right, left, right. . . . I couldn't get my long-irons to sit down softly on the greens, normally one of my strongest suits. Even my short swings were so rushed that I had very little touch or finesse around the green. I was like the businessman who wakes up an hour late, quickly shaves, showers, and dresses, races to the train, rushes into the office, and can't slow down for the rest of the day, with the result that he makes all kinds of mistakes. I played so erratically that by the sixth green I had lost the lead, and was five over par for the day at the turn. Down the stretch I managed to slow my swing to at least a manageable pace and hit some decent shots. But my better golf was way too little too late, and I finished a trailing and frustrated second.

From this distance, however, I value the educational impact of that experience. These days, I stop practicing with the driver once I have hit three good shots in a row. If I'm not fully satisfied with my swing, I might hit several more, but after that I play about a half-dozen short wedge shots to wind down my swing

Starting preround practice sessions by hitting easy wedge shots warms up my muscles gradually, while promoting good swing tempo and rhythm.

to its "serene" pace. Then I go over to the practice green to warm up my short game.

Thirty minutes, tops, is the total time I spend on bunker shots, chips, and putts prior to a tournament round. Any more and I tend to start taking these strokes for granted by losing concentration, which is a most dangerous attitude to take to the golf course.

To test the texture of the bunker sand, I hit a few shots from different lies. Basically, if the ball comes out low and "hot" from a normal lie, that tells me that the underbase is on the firm side, which means that during play I'll open the sand-wedge more than I would normally and hit a little more sharply downward to put some extra spin on the ball. If the texture is really hard, I might even play a pitching-wedge and make an extra-deep cut to extract the ball. When I produce extremely high shots with my normal steep-up-and-down technique, I know I'm in soft sand, so I'll set the blade of the sand-wedge square to very slightly open and try to make a very shallow cut of sand under the ball.

I get bored pretty quickly playing chip shots because this is one of the strongest parts of my game. Nevertheless, I invariably do play some long and short chips from the light and heavy fringes with a variety of clubs, with the main purpose of letting the ball's flight and roll tell me how "cute" I can be, or need to be, out on the course.

So far as putting practice goes, I usually get a sufficiently clear reading of the speed of the greens just by stroking a few fairly long uphill and downhill putts. After those, I practice mainly the four-foot "knee-knockers" that so often make or break the score. I'm normally a "die" putter who prefers to ease the ball to the hole. However, when the greens are either super-slick or super-slow, I change my strategy to a firmer stroke, particularly on short, breaking putts to prevent the ball from falling off-line or coming up short of the hole.

OTHER PRACTICE

Ordinarily, I go directly to the practice tee after every round, regardless of whether I've had a good or a bad day. However, I will pass up the postround session when I'm either physically tired or very fed up mentally, because I know how easily a fault can sneak into my swing if I tinker with my technique too much in such circumstances. Consequently, I believe that the players who obsessively go from the last green to the practice area without fail often do themselves more harm than good there.

Never neglect practicing some "knee-knockers" before a round because those are the shots that finally make or break your score.

I never practice just for the sake of practicing. My philosophy is this: If for some reason I'm unable to put 100 percent effort into my practice, I am better off passing and just making some mental notes, or actually writing down specific swing problems. Then I can return the next day, ready and raring to work even harder at my game.

Sometimes, a swing thought will just pop into my head seemingly out of nowhere when I'm on the practice tee, but, although it makes perfect sense theoretically, won't work physically. That's my cue to go back to the hotel room and relax, because often in the middle of watching a movie or doing some yoga I'll get a brainstorm that solves the problem.

I always practice with a definite purpose in mind, and when I accomplish it I stop. When my swing is fundamentally sound, I work on a weak department of my game, or practice a specific shot that I know I will have to play often on a particular upcoming course. For example, the greens at Augusta National are undulating and lightning-fast, so ahead of the Masters I spend hours on the putting green working on pace and line, perhaps moving the ball around in different stances until I find a position that feels so comfortable and secure I begin to believe I'll never miss the hole again. However, such keys usually change from day to day simply because one's mood and metabolism change.

The U.S. Open courses are always set up with very heavy rough along the fairways and around the greens. To prepare for that, I practice all kinds of recovery shots, both long and short, from similar rough. Wind plays the major role on many European courses, particularly at the British Open, which is always played on seaside links, so for that I'll focus my practice sessions around various techniques to handle breezes. Also, bunkers at British Opens are usually very severe—pot-shaped and high-lipped and deep—so I test wedges of various shapes and lofts, and practice with them from situations I expect to find in the championship itself.

Practicing tricky shots like this prepares you for unexpected on-course situations.

I practice hardest when I'm home in Pedreña on a break from tournament golf, the length and style of the sessions depending on how I'm playing at the time. If I'm relatively pleased with my game, I'll work on keeping things from getting rusty by rehearsing my entire preswing routine, repeatedly going through the fundamentals of grip, stance, aim, and alignment. When I swing, I always try very hard to *feel* my body working, so that I have muscle memory to fall back on if my technique should falter down the road.

When my swing is smooth and the shots do what I want them to, I tend to get bored, so then I'll break up my practice by playing the course, creating challenges for myself by pretending I have to shoot a particular score to win a major championship, or by playing the entire round with one club. After lunch, I might go back to the grind, practicing my short game on Pedreña's pitch-and-putt course, often until darkness sets in.

If I'm in a slump, things take on a different perspective. Then I will let my imagination run wild by experimenting with different ball positions, stances, clubface and body alignments, until I either regain my swing feel or stumble onto a new key. When I think I've identified a fault, I like to tackle it head on. For example, weak shots that fade from left to right are a sure sign that I'm swinging too slowly—a fault that prevents me from driving my legs and swinging my arms freely and fluidly enough in the downswing to deliver the clubface square at impact. To get more life into my motion, I'll put a dozen balls about a foot apart in a straight row, then step up along the row and hit them one after the other without stopping.

I've described my practice routines in detail, both as a general guideline and also to suggest that even good players only remain proficient at the game through constant work. Grabbing your driver and rushing to the range once a week to bang out a bucket of balls as hard and fast as you can is *not* what practice is all about.

Practicing productively involves constantly grooving the fundamentals that govern the swing, rehearsing the preswing routine, reinforcing good postural habits, constantly reviewing vital keys, and much more. For instance, hitting balls with your favorite club before play induces confidence, as does learning to hit your *least* favorite club—*after* the round. Practicing out of divots, off hilly and perched lies, off leaves and pine needles, under and over trees, off moist and dry turf, and all the other goofy situations you invariably encounter in golf, prepares you for both the expected and the unexpected. Chipping with a variety of clubs makes you a more versatile short-game player, while putting with your eyes closed teaches you to be more stroke-conscious than hole-conscious.

Practicing right also means hitting shots in all wind conditions, and out of bad and good lies in the sand and rough. It means learning how to fade the ball if you normally hit a draw, and drawing the ball if you normally hit a fade. Practice also means having the guts to stick with a new swing key on the course, even though you may not initially hit the ball accurately or powerfully. But, most of all, practice spells sacrifice. *Going to the range a little more and to the course a little less is the only true path to shooting the kind of golf you dream about.* Believe me: Practice really does pay off in the end in this game.

THE BALL-FLIGHT TEACHER

During my preround practice, I pay close attention to the flight characteristics of the ball on full shots, and to the way the ball rolls on chips and putts. Any dramatic change from normal indicates some fault in my setup, swing, or stroke. I know my game so well that I can generally identify the problem and correct it before I tee off.

Like many other players, I tend to slip into the same bad habits over and over again. For instance, pulling short-iron shots to the left tells me that I'm setting up with my hands behind the ball, a position that, for me, aligns the clubface left of the target line both at address and impact. Thus, moving my hands a little forward of the ball straightens the "pulls." When I repeatedly hit long-irons high and weakly, I immediately know that I'm "reverse-pivoting," leaning my upper body left on the backswing then rocking my weight to the right coming down, which causes me to hit up on the ball instead of with a sweeping motion. To correct it, I make an exaggerated effort to shift the majority of my weight to my right foot going back, without letting it roll to the outside of the foot, then to the left coming down.

Tee shots hit low and left tell me I'm setting up with my shoulders closed instead of square to the target, which makes me jut my right shoulder outward at the start of the downswing and hit over the top of the ball with a closed clubface.

Pushing putts consistently right of the hole is a sure sign I'm setting up with my hands too far in front of the ball, thereby aligning the blade right of where it should face at address. To correct, I reset my hands so that they are in line with the ball, with the back of my left hand square to the putterface and the starting line of the putt.

Unfortunately, I'll sometimes pick up a preround fault that totally baffles me. For instance, once in a while I get a case of the "fades" that minor adjustments in my setup or swing just won't cure. That's when I like to go and lay low, because long and hard experience has taught me never to start stripping my swing apart prior to play. These days, my thinking is: Why run the risk of modifying the action I've grooved over all these years when the problem could be due to nothing more than a little sluggishness on that particular day? So what I usually do is go ahead and simply play the entire round aiming the clubface a little bit left of my target to compensate for the left-to-right flight.

TEMPO DRILLS

My swing is based on a slowish tempo, a pace relaxed enough to permit me to time the movements of my body and the club in what I consider to be the correct sequence. When my tempo and timing are right, my entire swing feels effortless, particularly the forward motion. It feels as if it's being controlled by an outside agency, which I suppose is because a sound tempo allows especially the forward part of the swing to be entirely a reflexive action, as it must be to repeatedly produce fine golf shots.

Unfortunately, from time to time my tempo quickens and turns my swing sour. In the case of most amateurs, trying to hit the ball too hard is the usual cause of this problem, but in mine it is most often a reaction to the windy courses of Europe, where I play so much of my golf. In constant wind, my swing tends to become shorter and faster without my really realizing it. So, after each round, I go to work on what I believe to be the best of all "slow-down" drills: I pick a target 150 yards out and hit teed-up balls to it with the driver, the 3-iron, and the 5-iron, which encourages me to swing each club at essentially the same speed. After that, I'll often take a medium-iron and hit shots with my feet together, to make my arms more active and to remind my hands to serve as "quiet controllers" instead of "power generators."

After doing these drills, I know that my tempo has returned to normal if the distance I get from each of my clubs matches the distance I typically obtain under comparable course conditions.

CLUB SELECTION

I know the exact distance I normally get from each of my clubs—with a full or a three-quarter-length swing, with a slow or fast tempo, playing a draw or a fade or a low or high shot, hitting out of heavy or light rough, hitting off the fairway or off a tee, or in a headwind or tailwind, or in light or heavy air. Therefore, I can turn much of the strategic side of golf into an exercise in mathematics. Here, for example, are the clubs in my set and the average distance I *carry* each of them under normal course conditions, with my normal swing pace:

Club	*Carry*
Driver	250 yards
3-wood	235 yards
1-iron	220 yards
2-iron	210 yards
3-iron	200 yards
4-iron	190 yards
5-iron	180 yards
6-iron	170 yards
7-iron	160 yards
8-iron	150 yards
9-iron	140 yards
Pitching-wedge	130 yards
Sand-wedge	90 yards

There's no surer way to hit a bad shot than by being confused about club selection. My suggestion is that you spend enough time on the practice tee to learn your distances.

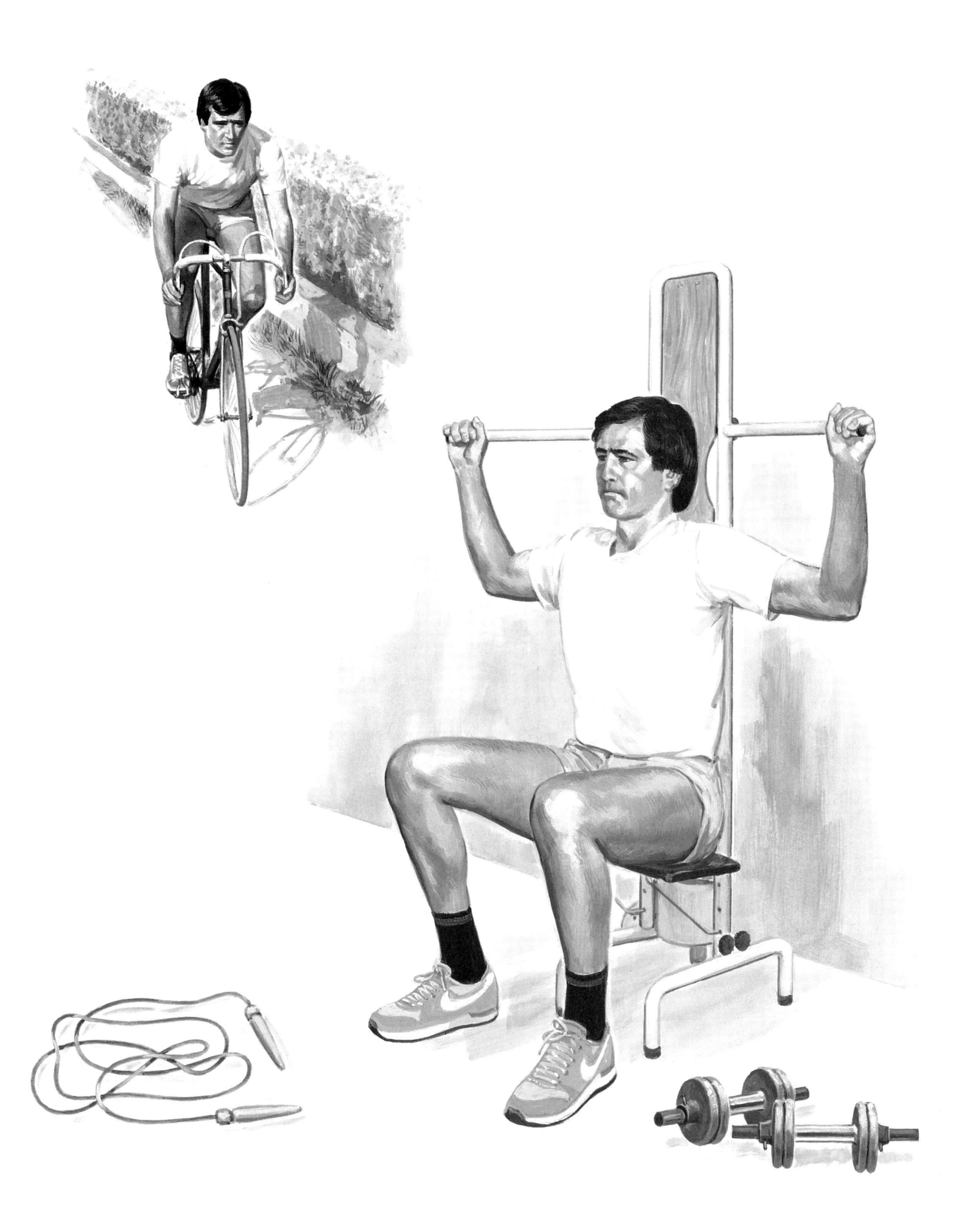

Chapter 14

LIVING RIGHT

No one who knows me well would accuse me of being a fitness nut, but I do adhere to a daily regimen of exercise and good nutrition, simply because I swing better and score lower when I'm in top shape. Even when I'm on the road, I do some light exercises when I get up each morning, just to get my heart pumping and to keep my muscles strong and limber. In the evening, I find that yoga breathing alleviates any tensions left over from that day's round and helps to relax me for eight hours of sound sleep.

At home in Spain, when taking time off from tournament play, I stick to the same morning exercise program, but also work out more intensely in my home gymnasium, using Nautilus equipment to build and sustain bodily strength. I don't overdo it, though—rather, I prefer to use the outdoors as my gymnasium. When I'm not practicing or playing golf at the Pedreña Golf Club, I swim, ride my racing bicycle hard through the winding hills of the surrounding countryside, shoot ducks and hunt rabbits, and play tennis, which is my favorite sporting pastime.

I took up tennis just a few years ago. I enjoy it because it takes less time than a round of golf, improves my flexibility and endurance, and gets my mind off golf. By my golfing standards, I'm about a twelve-handicap tennis player, but when I'm at La Manga (the Spanish golf club I represent) I play a few sets every day with some of the better players to try to keep up my competitive edge. I rarely win, but I am learning more about racquet control and strategy with each match—so look out, Jack Nicklaus!

As a youngster I had the proverbial ants in my pants, a tremendous amount of physical energy for things I enjoyed. Swinging a golf club, kicking a soccer ball, fishing, or just fooling around with my friends appealed to me a great deal more than doing my share of the chores on our family farm. Nevertheless, I got to be a pretty strong kid by picking corn, carrying animal feed, cleaning up the sheds, or just being a "gopher" for my father, and that strength contributes today to the precision and power in my swing. However, it wasn't until 1974 that I became conscious of the benefits of staying in shape, when I first got to know Gary Player. I was sulking in a corner of the locker room of South Africa's Wedgewood Park Country Club, after finishing fortieth in an event that Gary won. I was an immature, inexperienced, winless European tour rookie, and here comes this famous golfer who tells me I have the talent to be a world-beater, but that, unless I start paying attention to physical fitness, I will continue to tire in the late holes of a round, which will wreck my timing and tempo under pressure, as it had just done. I was a pretty headstrong teenager at that time, but I took Gary's advice and it was one of the smartest moves I ever made as a young professional.

Here are some of the ways I've discovered since then to get and keep myself fit for golf—and life.

The Legs

The legs must be strong to stabilize the winding and unwinding of the body on the back- and through-swings. When my legs feel strong, I feel strong all over, especially down the stretch.

Skipping rope is a simple, supreme leg toner, as well as being a fine heart-strengthening aerobic exercise. Also, jumping rope enhances my sense of balance and forces me to concentrate on timing and rhythm.

The Hips

Golf demands a uniquely strenuous rotary action of the hips, particularly on the downswing, so I work on strength, flexibility, and muscle memory by holding a five-pound dumbbell in my right hand, swinging up to the top and then, while firing my right side, vigorously swinging it down again. I go through this action, from takeaway to finish, ten to fifteen times per session.

The Hands, Wrists, and Forearms

Power and accuracy are both lost if the clubhead wobbles around during the swing. I constantly work to increase control by building up the muscles in my hands, wrists, and forearms.

To strengthen my hands, I squeeze a hard rubber ball about one hundred times, usually while I'm watching television or traveling on an airplane. Another good, simple exercise for toning the wrist and forearm muscles is to tie a five-pound weight to a rod, then hold the rod out chest high at arms' length with both hands and roll up the weight.

Nutrition

Basically, I stick to a diet of roughly 55 percent carbohydrates, 30 percent fats, and 15 percent proteins. I'm big on carbohydrates because they provide energy, and it takes a lot of energy to play seventy-two holes of tournament golf well, plus practice rounds, week after week. I eat carbohydrate-rich whole-grain cereals, strawberries, peaches, spinach, broccoli, peas, beans, potatoes, corn, rice, and pasta.

I used to think fat was to be avoided at all costs, but a nutritionist friend explained that fats are not only a main source of energy, but that they also provide essential vitamins. However, because excessive fat intake is harmful, I eat fish more often than red meat, steamed rather than fried vegetables, skimmed milk, and fresh fruit for dessert. I also stick to low-fat snacks such as raw vegetables, whole-grain crackers, or plain yogurt.

I never have to worry about eating right when I'm at home, because both my mother and my girlfriend are good cooks and constant campaigners against junk food. In my opinion, Spanish food is the most nutritious there is. The world of hot-dog stands, hamburgers, Chinese take-outs, and ice-cream stores is foreign to us, and, frankly, I hope it stays that way. Spaniards eat a big, healthy breakfast, a soup- or salad-type lunch, and a late but light dinner, which makes perfect sense to me. Also, the pace of life is slower in my country, so we relax when we eat our meals, taking time to thoroughly chew and digest our food.

Adjusting to foreign food is still a problem for me. I've heard that a top American tennis player had White Castle hamburgers flown from New York to England on the Concorde when he played Wimbledon. I always look for good Spanish restaurants in the places I compete, and, when I can't find one in the Yellow Pages, I stick to fish, fowl, fiber, fruit, and fresh vegetables, or cook myself a Spanish omelet, or buy a Spanish TV dinner.

Here are a few of my typical daily menus:

At Home

Breakfast: Omelet or scrambled eggs, whole-wheat toast, granola with fresh fruit such as bananas or berries, orange juice, one cup of decaffeinated coffee.

Lunch: Sopa de pescado (fish soup) or tapas (tidbits of clams, mussels, and other shellfish). Fresh fruit such as apples and pears. Aqua sin gas (noncarbonated mineral water).

Dinner: Paella (shellfish, squid, vegetables, saffron rice), or chicken, or freshly caught fish (sole and hake are my favorites), or occasionally veal. With any meal, Spanish tortilla (a cake of diced and fried potatoes, onions, and garlic in an egg batter).

On the Road

Breakfast: Pear, apple, banana, and orange mixed in a blender, soft-boiled egg, whole-wheat toast, glass of skimmed milk or decaffeinated coffee.

Lunch: Minestrone soup, mixed salad (no dressing), slices of Swiss cheese, ham, salami, and several glasses of mineral water. Fresh strawberries or peaches.

Dinner: Broiled trout, fresh spinach, asparagus, boiled potato, mineral water, occasionally a glass of red wine or beer, sometimes mixing the beer with a lemon- or lime-flavored soft drink (rather like the refreshing British drink called a "shandy").

44

Chapter 15

THE MIND AND GOLF

At least a couple of times a week I will overhear amateur golfers talking about whether the game is mostly mental or mostly physical. To me, the answer is crystal clear. Once you have ingrained an effective and repeatable full swing, and learned a reasonable repertoire of shots including an all-around reliable short game, golf is played almost entirely between your ears. And the better you hope eventually to play the game, regardless of your handicap now, the more you'll need to develop your mental strengths—confidence, concentration, courage, and common sense.

I think it was on the inward nine of the 1980 Masters at Augusta National that the importance of the mental side of golf really had its first great impact on me. Holes ten, twelve, and thirteen, so beautiful yet so dangerous, became a stumbling block for me. In fact, playing them turned into one big head game.

After scoring 66-69-68 for a 203 total and a seven-shot lead with one round to go, I increased the margin by three strokes on Sunday with a 33 on the outward nine. Then the wheels fell off, as a three-putt from 25 feet at the tenth hole initiated a streak of silly mental errors. I hit before I was sure of what club to play on the short par-three twelfth, and paid a severe price, pushing my tee shot into water guarding the green, and ending up with a double bogey. On the next hole, I made too slow a swing on my second shot, hit the ball fat, and sent it sailing into Rae's

Creek, which cost me a bogey. When I looked up at the scoreboard, I was shocked to see that my once-so-substantial lead had been sliced to only three strokes: Indeed, I felt just like I imagine a boxer does when he's being counted out. Thus I had to work extra hard on settling myself down as I prepared for my tee shot at fourteen, and it was at that moment that I truly realized the significance of mind over matter.

In winning tournaments all over the world, I had been in trouble before, but I had never collapsed or "choked." Consequently, I had never had to learn how to pull myself up from the bottom of the barrel, which is what all the great players have been able to do when they have found themselves struggling mentally during a round. Some vivid memories of playing with Gary Player in the final round of the 1978 Masters was what helped me regain my determination.

Back then, in watching Gary burn up Augusta, I witnessed what many sportswriters consider to be one of the all-time greatest comebacks in golfing history. Starting the day seven strokes behind Hubert Green, who was the tournament leader, Gary steadily closed the gap and then, as it seemed to me, actually *willed* himself to victory. As he and I walked down the thirteenth fairway, he had pointed to the huge gallery surrounding the green up ahead and said, "Seve, those people don't think I can win, but you watch, I'll show them," and with a staggering display of mental maturity and fortitude, he did just that. In one of the most sensational finishes in the tournament's history, Gary scored seven birdies over the last ten holes, shot sixty-four, and won his third Masters. The whole thing left an indelible impression on me.

In 1980, recalling that spectacular comeback restored my own courage to the point of allowing me to stop worrying about losing and to start concentrating positively on just one shot at a time. Then, once I began to paint positive pictures of smooth swings and successful results in my mind's eye, the feeling of confidence I had enjoyed in the three previous rounds quickly returned. Winning took care of itself as I finished par-birdie-par-par-par.

CONFIDENCE

I think the best dictionary definition of confidence is *full trust*. Applied to golf, that means essentially this: When a player *thinks* he's going to hit a good shot, he usually will—provided, of course, that his positive attitude is realistically based on a sound swing and good shotmaking ability developed through regular and rigorous practice.

The harder you prepare for *anything*, the higher your level of confidence about it, thus the less pressure you feel, thus the better you perform. Relate this work ethic to practicing golf, as all fine players do, and you will definitely begin to play the game with a more positive attitude about hitting the shots it takes to be a winner. Eventually you'll even reach the point where you can think less about how to hit the ball and more about where to hit it, which is fundamental to fine scoring at every level of golf.

A vivid memory of Gary Player's remarkable comeback at Augusta in 1978 pushed me to turn my game around and win my first Masters in 1980. That experience, more than any other, taught me the true significance of mind over matter in golf.

CONCENTRATION

I began to acquire my powers of concentration long ago when learning to create a variety of shots with only my old 3-iron. I had to focus very intensely indeed on the grip, the setup, and the swing path to get the results I wanted out of that awkward, overlong club, and it taught me how to enter a mental cocoon which today insures that every shot I play gets my undivided attention. That's probably why I must "grind" for the entire round, unlike a Lee Trevino or a Fuzzy Zoeller, who can let up and laugh and joke between shots.

The key for me lies in always looking down an imaginary tunnel to my target. In doing so, I conjure up a clear picture of a perfectly played shot, then simply set myself into the appropriate address position to execute it. This process steadies my nerves, stops my mind from wandering, and blanks out all distractions. Try it in your game.

COURAGE

A friend of mine who trains dogs for a living told me a story that sheds some light on the subject of courage. He was called to the home of one of Spain's premier matadors, a bullfighter idolized for his *machismo* in the ring. The wife of this great man was pulling their German shepherd into the living room by a leash, when suddenly the dog broke loose and started barking and snarling as it ran wildly around the house. Well, I was sure my friend was going to tell how the bullfighter heroically wrestled the dog to the ground, but no—the matador jumped up on a table, quivering with fear!

What I'm saying is this: When a man of strong character leaves his element, he's often a weaker man. This theory seems to fit the game of golf. Many good golfers never live up to their full potential because they never learned the secrets of developing a courageous on-course attitude. These are the babies who throw clubs, continually cuss themselves out, sulk, or even walk off the course after one too many bad bounces or bad holes. Their problem is that they expect perfection, whereas the complete and intelligent—and courageous—golfer respects the game's unpredictability, takes it in stride, and gets on with the job as best he possibly can. Even when he's having an absolutely awful day, this player still gives every shot 100 percent concentration. His final score is his absolute best effort for that day, and biting the bullet like this hardens him for future rounds. Thus, in my opinion, courage is not inherited, but developed through a combination of experience, sheer grit, and determination.

As far as I'm concerned, Jack Nicklaus is still the world's most courageous player. Although I've felt this way for many years, I'll never forget his gutsy performance in the 1981 British Open, played at Royal St. George's.

Retreating into an impenetrable "bubble" of concentration works for my particular personality. However, if grinding relentlessly makes you tense, try relaxing between shots by escaping into nongolf shots—Trevino-style!

Before a tournament, especially a major, Jack puts in days of practice on the course, mapping out every nook and cranny, to the point where, by the time he tees it up for real, he knows the course as well as the back of his hand. That was the case with Royal St. George's, so he was pretty confident about the week. But no one knows better than Nicklaus how this game can turn sour, and he got a taste of it on opening day.

Jack shot eighty-three, his worst-ever score in a major championship. And here's what he told the press immediately after the round: "That was the best I could do today—I tried my best on every shot."

That's the nature of this great man, and also of all courageous players. And it enabled him to go out the next day and shoot a course-record sixty-six, after which he said: "I can still win this championship with two more rounds like today's."

What a fabulous attitude—and what a lesson for all golfers!

COMMON SENSE

I'm amazed at some of the foolish chances my amateur partners take in Pro-Ams, which frequently end up costing them an "X" on the hole. They would never dream of driving at 120 miles per hour, or gambling their life savings at a card table, yet on the golf course they seem unable to retain even an ounce of common sense.

During a typical round, every golfer runs into many situations in which he must decide whether to gamble or play safe. On a drive, he may have to decide whether to try to cut the corner of a dogleg to shorten the hole, or take the less risky line. On an approach, he will have to decide whether to fire at the flagstick and risk finding deep greenside trouble, or play it to the sure side and rely on his putter. Facing a twenty-footer fast and downhill, he has to make up his mind whether to be bold and maybe go well past if the ball misses the hole, or lag up into that imaginary three-foot circle surrounding the cup to ensure a two-putt. The list goes on, and some choices are much more testing than others, but the bottom line is the same every time: Playing with common sense involves making the decision to play aggressively or safely, based on a *realistic appraisal of one's capabilities*. And in doing that, the chief consideration should be the reward of pulling off the shot relative to the cost of missing it.

What this requires above all else, of course, is discipline—which just might be the most important word in the entire golfing lexicon.

Severiano Ballesteros: A Career Profile

Born: April 9, 1957, in Pedreña, Spain
Height: 6 feet
Weight: 175 pounds
Special interests: boxing, bicycling, soccer, tennis, shooting, chess
Turned professional: 1974
Attachments: La Manga Club, Spain

Major Championships

1979 British Open
1980 U.S. Masters
1983 U.S. Masters
1984 British Open
1988 British Open

Other Tournament Victories (Worldwide)

1976: Dutch Open
Lancome Trophy (France)

1977: French Open
Uniroyal International (U.K.)
Swiss Open
Japanese Open
Dunlop Phoenix (Japan)
Otago Classic (Japan)

1978: Greater Greensboro Open (U.S.A.)
Martini International (U.K.)
German Open
Scandinavian Enterprise Open (Sweden)
Swiss Open
Kenya Open
Japanese Open

1979: English Golf Classic

1980: Madrid Open
Martini International (U.K.)
Dutch Open

1981: Suntory World Match-play Championship (U.K.)
Australian PGA Championship
Scandinavian Enterprise Open (Sweden)
Benson & Hedges Spanish Open
Dunlop Phoenix (Japan)

1982: Suntory World Match-play Championship (U.K.)
Paco Rabanne French Open
Cepsa Madrid Open

1983: Westchester Classic (U.S.A.)
Carrolls Irish Open
Lancome Trophy (France)
Sun City Challenge (Bophuthatswana)
Sun Alliance PGA (U.K.)

1984: Suntory World Match-play Championship (U.K.)
Sun City Challenge (Bophuthatswana)

1985: USF & G Classic (U.S.A.)
Suntory World Match-play Championship (U.K.)
Carrolls Irish Open
Peugeot French Open
Sanyo Open (Spain)
Benson & Hedges Spanish Open (U.K.)

1986: Dunhill British Masters
Carrolls Irish Open
Johnnie Walker Monte Carlo Open
Peugeot French Open
KLM Dutch Open
Lancome Trophy (tied) (France)

1987: Master Suze Open (France)
Spanish PGA

1988: Open de Baleares (Mallorca)
Westchester Classic (U.S.A.)
Scandinavian Open (Sweden)
German Open

PGA European Tour Order of Merit Standings

Year	*Money**	*Standing*
1987	138,842	6
1986	259,275	1
1985	165,154	3
1984	142,577	5
1983	113,864	2
1982	74,617	10
1981	65,928	7
1980	52,090	3
1979	47,411	2
1978	54,348	1
1977	46,436	1
1976	39,504	1
1975	4,995	26
1974	2,915	118

*Pounds Sterling

International Appearances

Ryder Cup Team: 1979, 1983, 1985, 1987

In 1987, Ballesteros beat Curtis Strange, America's leading money winner, in a last-day singles match that clinched a historic first victory for the European team in America.

Dunhill Cup: 1985, 1986

Hennessy Cognac Cup: 1976, 1978

World Cup Team: 1975, 1976, 1977

Ballesteros won the cup in 1976, partnering Manuel Pinero, and in 1977 with Antonio Garrido.

Miscellaneous Highlights

European Tour Vardon Trophy Winner (leading player of the year): 1976, 1977, 1978, 1986.

Low Career Round: 61, Nissan Cup (Japan) 1984.

1984 BRITISH OPEN

1979 BRITISH OPEN

1988 BRITISH OPEN

1983 MASTERS

1980 MASTERS